THE IMPOSSIBLE JOURNEY TO REALITY

*How Cerebral Palsy
and God Created Blessings
in One Man's Life*

Joseph Ferreira

The Impossible Journey to Reality: How Cerebral Palsy and God Created Blessings in One Man's Life
Copyright © 2025 Joseph Ferreira

Produced and printed by Stillwater River Publications. All rights reserved. Written and produced in the United States of America. This book may not be reproduced or sold in any form without the expressed, written permission of the author and publisher.

Visit our website at
www.StillwaterPress.com
for more information.

First Stillwater River Publications Edition.

ISBN: 978-1-965733-82-0 (*hardcover*)
ISBN: 978-1-965733-84-4 (*paperback*)

1 2 3 4 5 6 7 8 9 10
Written by Joseph Ferreira.
Cover & interior book design by Matthew St. Jean.
Cover photograph by Benjamin / Adobe Stock.
Back cover & spine photographs provided by Joseph Ferreira.
Published by Stillwater River Publications,
West Warwick, RI, USA.

The views and opinions expressed in this book are solely those of the author and do not necessarily reflect the views and opinions of the publisher.

Dedication

I dedicate this book to:

1) My faith in my Almighty God; without Him, I'm nothing. I was created by Him to show others that you don't have to be born perfect. He has a path of life that He has set for you. Continue and do not stray from this journey. Your journey can be lonely at times; however, it will take you to incredible places, and you will meet amazing people along the way. Someone will be there for you to pick you up, dust you off, pat you on the back, and point you in the right direction. I am convinced that even the people that you meet for a split second have an impact on your life. People say there are no more miracles—well, I see miracles every day. Because I know that God holds your last breath in His hands.

2) My family, who are the major core of my life. I could not ask for a better family. When I realize and reflect upon them, they were chosen for me and vice versa. Everyone and everything has a purpose in life under God. Without my family, I would be institutionalized and forgotten, I would not be a husband nor a father, and I certainly would not have had the opportunities to meet so many dear people throughout my

life. Every day has been a gift, and it is one gift that keeps on giving.

3) My friends and acquaintances whom I have met in my life. If I were able to list every friend that I have made, this book would never be completed. For those people who call me a friend, let me take this opportunity to say thank you because, without you, I would be lost. You were the ones who picked me up, dusted me off, and walked with me in my path of life. Lou Gehrig, one of the greatest baseball players of all time, had a famous quote. "If you find one good friend in a lifetime, then you are the luckiest man alive." Well, Mr. Gehrig, I found many good friends in my life, so I guess I really am one of the luckiest men alive.

If you replace the word "luckiest" with "blessed," then you have it correct. The word lucky can be a dog's name, so I say that I replace the word "lucky" with the word "blessed."

GOD + FAMILY + FRIENDS = MY SUCCESS

I have Cerebral Palsy. I am writing this book to show others that just because I have a disability, it does not mean that I cannot live a "normal" life. I hope that my readers will see that they can do anything they put their minds to.

The Impossible Journey to Reality

Part One

1

When I was born, the part of my brain that controls my physical abilities got damaged due to a lack of oxygen. The things that were affected were my ability to walk, the use of my right hand, and my speech. My disabilities are not caused by heredity. My parents had three more children, and thank God, all three of them were born physically normal. My mental capabilities function very well.

I was born on September 29, 1958, in a small village in São Miguel, Azores, Portugal. I am the oldest of four sons. My mother had a hard labor with me. My parents couldn't afford to deliver me in a hospital, so I was born at home and was delivered by a neighbor who delivered babies for many in my village. During the delivery, they thought I was going to die because when I was coming out of my mother's womb, I turned many different colors. They thought I wasn't going to make it, but they did not give up fighting for my life.

For the first four months, I kept my parents up day and night. They took me to the doctors constantly with no positive results, and they spent money that they often didn't have. No one could tell them what was wrong with me. The doctors first diagnosed me as being mentally challenged and, later, as having polio.

At the time, my father was a fisherman, and when the bad weather came, he didn't go out onto the water. That meant he didn't earn any money. Back then, in Portuguese culture, men were expected to be the breadwinners, and women were expected to stay home, bear children, and take care of the domestic chores. Those women who were barren were considered cursed. In those days, having a good family meant having a large family. My mother wasn't allowed to work, but it was a blessing because she devoted all her time to me.

On December 25, 1959, my brother Michael was born. Since it was Christmastime, my parents automatically thought it was a gift from God. To this day, I really believe Michael was the key to unlocking some of the mysteries and questions that my parents had about my developmental health. As my brother learned how to crawl and then walk, I couldn't even sit up properly. My parents tell me that they used to stack up pillows and put them on either side just to keep me sitting up. I remember my brother walking and running, and I could only wonder when it would be my turn.

On May 27, 1961, my brother Thomas was born. He, too, was born healthy and progressed normally. As they grew, my brothers used to play together, and I would watch. I really didn't mind because, for some reason, I knew in my heart that I would one day be joining them.

My father was studying to be a postal worker, and after months of studying for his exam, he was finally offered a job in my village. This new and prestigious job meant a whole different lifestyle for my parents and me because I could get better care from the city doctors rather than the village doctor.

Everyone who worked with my father shared his pain about having a handicapped child. Someone at the post office told my father about a hospital in Lisbon that strictly dealt with handicapped children. Going there meant that I would be away from my family for a long period of time, and that didn't sit too well with my parents. However, it was the only option they really had because no matter where they sought help for my condition, they ran out of resources.

There seemed to be two choices: either that I go and try to get better, or they could continue to second-guess each other, saying, "What if...?" My parents made the right decision—they let me go—with reluctance, of course. My parents normally wouldn't have been able to afford it, but because my father worked for the postal service, my parents only paid twenty percent of the bill. So, I was off to Lisbon. Before I left my family, our mother gave birth to my third brother, Victor. He was born on September 17, 1962.

I remember my mother carrying me while my father walked beside her as we headed to the ship that would take me to the hospital in Lisbon. When we got to the cargo ship, my parents did not want to give me up, especially my mother. My mother is a wonderful lady. She isn't the most educated person, but she is full of great love and understanding, not only for me but also for those around her. It broke her heart to have me leave her. All three of us were crying, but finally, they relinquished me to the two ladies who had agreed to take care of me on the journey. I found out later that these two ladies were nuns whom my parents had found by chance. They really took very good care of me and treated me like their own son. I also remember them praying for me, asking God to please let me walk.

2

After two weeks at sea, I arrived at St. Jose Hospital in Lisbon to begin a long process of physical therapy. The hospital there had a very good reputation for crippled children. They never turned anyone away for any reason. They were very loving and caring, and they really made me feel right at home. For the next few months, they were my family. I can't begin to thank them enough for what they did for me.

After my orientation, we went right to work. At the age of four, I had never seen so many doctors and nurses. After breakfast, I would start my therapy. Everything was new to me; I had never tried anything like this before. I was terrified and would cry. The staff was very patient with me. The nurses hugged and kissed me constantly. When I couldn't do a particular task, they encouraged me to try just a little bit harder. There was one therapist by the name of Cathy who always greeted me in the morning with a big hug. Cathy encouraged me by saying, "You are going to walk today!" I believe to this day that I understood what it was to have courage for the first time because they pushed me to the limit. The bravery I learned while at St. Jose's was the seed that formed the courage and determination that have been with me my whole life.

My parents kept in contact with the hospital constantly,

and the doctors kept sending them positive feedback. Even though it was a slow process, I was getting better with each passing day. Therapy began to be fun, and I used to look forward to the therapy sessions. I believe that when things become fun, it is easier to master them. Sometimes, though, frustration would set in when I couldn't do a particular task. I felt everything that I touched had to be perfect, and the things that bothered me the most were the simple tasks, tasks that I felt deep down in my heart I should be able to do, but because of my disability, I couldn't.

After being at St. Jose Hospital for two months, I was experiencing most of my body parts moving for the first time. It was both scary and exciting. It was great to feel my legs getting stronger because I had never experienced anything like that before in my life. The doctors and nurses also saw the progress that I was making, and they pushed me just a little bit harder each day, and the more they pushed, the more I wanted to be pushed.

I also made a lot of friends there. We used to get into a lot of mischief together—nothing bad, but we pulled our pranks, especially with the doctors and nurses. One time, we decided to rearrange our room. You can just envision handicapped children trying to become interior decorators; it was just a riot! When someone couldn't do a certain thing, we all would pitch in. I guess that's why we got along so well together; we all had something in common, and there was a special bond between each one of us. Because I was so far from home, they were the closest things that I had to a real family, and as far as I was concerned, they were my family.

There was a man there who was in his mid-fifties that I adopted as my father. All of us children called him "Daddy." He was one of the sweetest men I had met and was truly the father figure that I needed. Just his warm smile made me feel relaxed. He helped me in so many ways. He gave me words of encouragement and strength to go on, and always told me to be patient because I would be walking someday. If I did something wrong, he would correct me in a loving way.

Sure enough, I finally began to walk! I was using a walker. It was a slow process, but I was walking. Each day, my legs were getting stronger and stronger. It was a totally different feeling, and each step I took was a new experience. The more I walked, the more I wanted to walk. I felt that walking was too good to be true, and I didn't know if or how long I'd be able to have this newly found freedom. So, every chance I got, all I did was walk with my walker.

I had been at the hospital for nine months, and the progress I had made was tremendous. The doctors and the nurses worked miracles with me, and they deserve a lot of credit for my physical appearance. Those nine months were just the whole key to my future. At this time, the staff felt I was ready to go back home. They told my parents that I was going to come back walking; however, I would need a walker, and that even though I was walking, I would never walk like a normal person.

Saying goodbye is often the toughest thing that anyone must do. I had made a lot of friends, and each one of them meant a lot to me. I just didn't want to leave because I was so comfortable there. It was time to go and reenter my community at home.

3

When I got back to my village in São Miguel, naturally, everybody wanted to see me. It was great seeing everybody, especially my family. I came back with my trusty walker; to me, that was my best friend in the whole world, and without it, I couldn't survive. Slowly but surely, I kept making progress on my own with my parents watching.

I was always an early riser, and in the morning, I would go to my grandmother's house, across the street. She gave me a nickname; she used to call me "the rooster," because the rooster would wake up everybody, and I was up with the sun, moving about. It was a joy just to be walking on my own without bothering anybody.

My brothers, even though they were younger than I, always helped me. Whatever I wanted to do, they would help without any questions. I had a second walker that needed two people to maneuver it. My brother Michael would grab the front end, and I would grab the back end, and he would lug me around. One day, I saw other children running, and I wanted to try it. I told my brother to run with the walker as fast as he could. That was the first time I ever ran in my life, so of course, my brother and I did it every day for about two weeks! People began to complain because we would go into the street, and cars would come fast around the corner. In Europe, even to this day, people like to go fast. The neighbors were afraid that we would get hit by a car! My parents would talk to my brother and me, but that didn't do any good—all I wanted to do was to run. It lasted two more weeks, and people continued to complain. My parents again talked to us, and again that didn't do any good. The more my parents talked to me, the more I wanted to run. I felt free.

One day, early in the morning, I went to get my walker, and to my surprise, I found that someone had broken one of the legs on it. To me, that was one of the meanest things that anyone could ever do. I cried for days, and I couldn't even eat. I tried to find out who did it, but I could not. It wasn't until I heard my parents talking that I learned that my father had broken it to keep me from running in the street. I was very angry at my father because he took my independence away from me. I couldn't understand that, because I really thought my parents wanted me to walk on my own.

I had to use the smaller walker, so my brother could not make it go fast and help me run anymore. I was very attached to that one, because without it, I couldn't take another step; I would just flop to the ground.

My brothers, who all walked normally, always took me with them, no matter where they went. When the kids from the neighborhood got together to play, I always tagged along. My brothers didn't let the fact that I was disabled separate us. They always treated me as an equal. They also made sure that the rest of the kids knew about it.

My brothers were also wise; even at a young age, they knew my limitations. When there was something I couldn't do, they would sit me down under a tree and I would watch them playing. I really didn't mind, because somehow, I felt that I was still a part of my brothers while they were playing.

Don't get me wrong; at times it did bother me, but not very often. Oh, how I would long to be like anyone else running and playing. I knew that wasn't possible then, but I just knew deep down in my heart I would be doing it someday. At this time, all I could do was admire the others.

In the meantime, my parents kept in contact with the doctors back in Lisbon. My parents told them that I was too attached to my walker. The doctors insisted that my parents take away the walker because the doctors feared that I would rely on it too much. When my parents took the doctor's advice, I felt betrayed, because they had taken away my only way of getting around. Since I didn't have my walker, I just sat around the house. My parents encouraged me to go out and play with the other kids, but I refused because my equalizer was gone.

4

The doctors suggested that my parents try a different method, which was simply to have either one or both of them take my hand and start walking. I really enjoyed that because I had support on either side. I really didn't mind where we went if they took me. One day, my father had some business to take care of, and I wasn't allowed to go with him. Unfortunately, there wasn't anyone available that day to help me walk, so I just sat around the house all day and cried. I was afraid to do anything on my own for fear that I might get hurt. If I fell, who would help me get to my feet?

The Portuguese have a tradition: Sundays are usually visiting days, when everybody gathers around someone's house. One Sunday, I noticed a very large gathering at our house. I looked at my father and asked him why so many people were there, because it was unusual to see that many people at our house at one time. He looked at me and smiled and said, "They came over to see you walk." Every blood relative you could think of was there, and a few friends on top of that.

As my father and I were walking, he had my left hand, and my right hand was on the house for extra support. I noticed my father slowly inching away from the house—I really didn't mind because he had the other hand. I was far enough from the house that I couldn't reach it. What I feared the most happened—my father let go of my hand. I tried to reach for my father, but he was out of my reach. I told my father that without him, I couldn't move. I started to cry, and then he cried too. He told me, "If you don't do it now, you will never do it." He and everybody who was there began to encourage me and urged me to take that first step on my own.

I took a step and then I fell, but what surprised everyone was that I got up and tried again and again. I guess the more times I fell, the more I was determined to do it over and over. The seeds of courage and determination that had been planted at St. Jose began to take root and flourish.

Day after day, Michael, Thomas, and Victor tried to help me in every way that they could. Even though they treated me as their equal, my brothers basically were my shields, and they protected me from bullies and unkind people. I can't explain it, but for some reason, it was embedded in their hearts. When the other kids made fun of me, my brothers would get into a fight on my behalf. One day, my brother Victor and I were walking, and some kid pushed me, and I fell to the ground. Victor chased him and beat him up. My brothers really tried very hard to make me comfortable and happy. They seemed to realize that I was different from them and that just because I was disabled, I still participated in their activities.

I had the best of both worlds; my brothers treated me as their equal, and my parents gave me everything. My parents did so much for me; they gave me the best life. They tried to get me the best doctors, medication, and experiences. They really went overboard with me. As I got older, I felt guilty because I believed that they gave me too much attention, which took it away from my brothers, and that really bothered me.

Every time new doctors came around the area, my parents

would make an appointment so the doctor could see me. They were hoping for a miracle drug, but unfortunately, there wasn't any. My parents would not even care about the cost; sometimes, they would borrow it just to pay for the consultation. Doctors and other practitioners back then believed in using a lot of "natural" methods to treat various ailments. The village "medicine man" told my parents to take me to the river and hit my legs with a prickly leaf, and then dunk my legs into salt water. The theory was that by opening my skin with the prickly leaf, it would soak up the salt water and cure me. Another doctor told my parents to apply an electric shock to the soles of my feet. They used paddles that were wired to a machine, and shocked my feet every week for three months, until finally they realized it wasn't working. You must understand that back then in Portugal, they weren't advanced in technology.

5

When I turned seven (that was the age when kids went to school), each teacher visited my house to meet me. They naturally had questions for my parents as well. After talking to me and my parents, they decided it was best for me to stay home. Even though I had the mental capabilities, they were afraid that I would get hurt physically. The teachers were concerned that, being the only handicapped student there, they didn't have the money to hire a special teacher for me. Back then, the schools in Portugal were not accommodating to the handicapped population. Basically, handicapped people were not allowed to go to school, mostly due to concerns about safety. As a member of a minority, you didn't have the same rights as the other children did.

My mother had a sister in America, and she was trying to get us to move there. My parents weren't sure the Portuguese government would allow me to leave Portugal because if there was something wrong with you, you weren't allowed to go to another country. My mother told my father that if I wasn't allowed to go, she would stay with me, and my father would go with the other three boys. Fortunately, I was allowed to go to the United States. I still wonder if my parents did a little hanky panky to get permission for me to come to America.

Whatever they did, I am grateful; coming to America was the best thing that could have ever happened to me.

Finally, on June 10, 1966, we came to America. I was then not quite eight years old. As I remember, when we arrived in Boston at Logan Airport, the weather was terrible. The trip itself was awful due to bad weather. I remember passengers giving thanks to God for reaching their destination. My aunt and her family were waiting for us at the airport, and we stayed with them for three months while my parents looked for work.

That summer, when we arrived in America, my aunt registered the three oldest boys to go to school in the fall. Michael, Thomas, and I went to public school, but Victor wasn't allowed to go because he was too young. It was a new experience for me because back in Portugal, I wasn't allowed to attend. In the United States, every child up to the age of sixteen must attend school. That is one thing this wonderful country gives you. You can be anything that you want to be—you are the only one to put limitations on yourself. I was enrolled in ALS classes right away to learn English. I had a wonderful teacher there by the name of Ms. Camera, who took me under her wing. I think that because I was disabled, she gave me extra attention. I was eager to learn the language, and with her support, I picked up English rather quickly. The first word that I learned was the word "clock." Ms. Camera had a watch on her wrist, and she asked the class, "What's this on my wrist?" I raised my hand and I answered, "clock." She said that I had given her the wrong answer, and I was totally confused. She looked at me and said, "Joe, you are partially right, but the correct word is 'watch.'"

All of us had lunch boxes. One day, I ate my lunch, and I went to put my lunchbox away. I tripped and hit the right side of my head near the temple. I didn't make a big deal, and

I went to the boy's room and grabbed a paper towel. I went to class ten minutes later, and Ms. Camera saw me wiping my head with the paper. She immediately contacted the nurse, who in turn contacted my father. I was sent to the Bristol Medical Center. I required thirty stitches on my head, which needed to heal. I couldn't return to school for two weeks. When I came back to school, I was more than ready to learn all that I needed to pass that year.

The school had a dilemma because they did not know where they would put me the following year. If they put me in a regular public school, I might fall and get hurt again. It was decided that I was to go to a school for handicapped children called Meeting Street School.

6

When September rolled along, I began school at Meeting Street. I had a wonderful teacher by the name of Ms. Cameron, who was very caring and loving. I started first grade two years older than the other kids in my class. Coming from another country at a young age, not only did I have to learn a different lifestyle and culture, but a different language as well. I was able to pick up some English rather quickly. I guess when you are surrounded by people who only speak one language, you can't help but pick it up. I liked school right away because Meeting Street School had a lot of students in the same situation that I was in. I was able to be on par with my peers, and they were able to compete with me. It was at Meeting Street School that I finally received the correct diagnosis for my condition. I had cerebral palsy, not mental retardation and not polio.

I believe the first friend that I made was a student by the name of Billy (Moose) Gordon. Billy also had cerebral palsy; maybe that's why I drew closer to him. He helped me a lot, especially in communication; he would correct my English. He and I would help each other in any way that we could. I guess he and I complemented each other—whatever I couldn't do, he would do, and vice versa.

I excelled in my academic work; my favorite subject was math. I loved to do addition, subtraction, etc. The teachers noticed my positive progress and my positive attitude. I was always willing to try to do something different, and I was always asking questions as to when certain things worked and why they didn't work.

I had a physical therapist named Mr. Marshall. He was a wonderful human being. He always told me, "If you want it badly enough, you will get it." He was patient enough to follow me through every exercise that he wanted me to learn. He also corrected me on the things that I did wrong. I still remember his voice saying, "It seems you always put a lot of effort into the things that you enjoy, but you don't put any effort into things that you don't enjoy." Even though I was walking, he strengthened my legs and arms, and he made my body more mobile with each passing day.

My favorite person was Mr. John Oliver, my personal driver. Each morning, he would pick Billy and me up for school and take us home in the afternoons. Mr. Oliver was an important male role model for me...I believe I called him "Paizinho" ("Daddy") on more than one occasion. He was one of the kindest men that you could ever meet. He always gave me only words of inspiration and kind words. Mr. Oliver noticed that we didn't have a lot of money, so every Friday after school, he would take Billy and me to McDonald's or Dairy Queen.

I completed six months at Meeting Street School. I think my success in academics forced them to let me go to public school, because I went to the first grade in regular school in the middle of the year. The school put me into the special education class because I had not picked up the English language well enough to be in a regular classroom. I kept asking, "Where is Billy?" because I thought at the time that he and

I were supposed to stay together. Unfortunately for me, he stayed at Meeting Street School.

In second grade, my teacher's name was Mrs. Carr. She was a sweet lady who tried to make me feel at home with her warm smile. However, I was scared because I was the only disabled student there. I wasn't completely comfortable in class, and no matter what Mrs. Carr said or did, I couldn't adjust. Mrs. Carr sat me down next to a girl by the name of Mary Lou O'Brien, who smiled at me and tried to make me feel at home. Unfortunately, that didn't work either. All I kept asking her was when Billy was coming. Naturally, she didn't know what was going on, but she did hang around to watch over me.

At recess, I was always alone because the students didn't know how to react towards me. Besides, I was still looking for Billy with no success. I tried to make friends, but the kids shied away from me. At the time, I was the only disabled student; plus, there was the fact that the parents told their children to stay away from strangers. I finally gave up hope of looking for Billy. I just wanted to make friends in any way.

I would have done anything to make a friend. My father used to give us a quarter a week to buy a small container of milk each day at lunch. Instead of drinking my milk, I drank water because I gave the quarter to a fellow student at recess and told him I would give him a quarter a week if he would be my friend—naturally, he agreed.

A couple of weeks went by, and the teacher's aide noticed me drinking water and reported it to my teacher. My teacher called my parents in. My father came in because my mother was working the first shift (my father worked the second shift). She told my father that if he couldn't afford the milk, the school would pay for it. My father explained that even though our family was poor, he gave his sons a quarter a week for milk. They told my father that I wasn't drinking milk, that

I was drinking water! The teachers called me into the office. When I saw my father there, I was very surprised. My teacher asked me why I wasn't drinking milk at lunchtime. I told her that I couldn't say, and that someone had asked me to keep it a secret. My father asked me what happened to the quarter that he had given me at the beginning of the week. I didn't want to tell him either, but he forced it out of me. I told the truth about giving my quarters to my classmate, and to my surprise, there wasn't a dry eye in the office. They couldn't believe that I would go to such an extreme to make a friend.

7

Mrs. Carr talked to the class about friendship following the meeting in the office. That lecture was the key to me making friends. Afterwards, I was able to get closer to the other kids. I have been lucky because I have always had an outgoing personality. Once they gave me a chance, I made new friends every day. Instead of being alone at recess, now I had a flock around me.

My peers were very understanding and soon were trying to help me in any way that they could, and I tried to do the same. I developed a good relationship with my fellow students. If a stranger made fun of me, they would stick up for me. Now, at recess, I was the most popular person; everyone wanted to be with me. I really didn't mind it—in fact, I loved every minute of it! But even though I had friends, more than I knew what to do with, I still felt like an outsider looking in. Having cerebral palsy, I didn't have too many things other than school in common with kids my age.

One thing that was exceptional was that my grades were above anyone's expectations, especially considering my disability. I always wanted to learn and constantly asked questions if I wasn't certain about something. I was always happy to help my fellow classmates whenever they needed my assistance. In fact,

Mrs. Carr always recommended me to anyone who needed help with their work. I had fellow students come up to me and ask for tutoring, and I was more than willing to be available to someone in need. If someone needed my help, I didn't care when or where, I would try to help him or her. It made me feel valued and that I was contributing.

Recess was getting more and more fun because in the spring, it was baseball season. The interesting part was that whoever picked me on their team, that team would get an extra out. So naturally, everyone wanted me on their team. The kids would fight over me, and that felt good.

I always loved sports, and when I found out the other boys were signing up for Little League, I just had to sign up. When they saw me, the league officials wouldn't allow me to play because of the limitations caused by my cerebral palsy. I wasn't angry, but I was sad because I wasn't allowed to play the game that I loved. This is about the time it was beginning to dawn on me that I couldn't do the things I enjoyed the most because of my cerebral palsy, like baseball, football, basketball, and hockey. By the same token, deep down in my heart, I still believed that as I got older, my cerebral palsy would disappear, and someday I would be like every normal kid. I tried not to let it get me down too much, and just waited for that moment when I would be like everyone else.

My brothers, Michael and Thomas, signed up to play Little League like the other kids and were put on the same team. What followed was an example of compassion that I will never forget as long as I live. The manager of their team, John Marino, knew my situation, and he made me the batboy. It was the thrill of my life. I even got a complete uniform. The team would practice about three times a week. After practice, Coach Marino would get the team together, and they would let me bat for about fifteen minutes. Even though I couldn't play in a regular game because of my cerebral palsy, he still gave me time after practice. Before every game, my brother Thomas and I would go to church and say a little prayer that we might win that game. I remember Coach Marino looking at me and saying, "Joe, did you go to church today?" And I would reply, "Yes, I did, Coach." That year, we almost won the World Series, but we came in second. It was a wonderful experience for me as a kid who wanted to feel included, and I will always remember Coach Marino for his kindness. It was one of the most special times of my young life.

My brothers continued to play a major role in my life, just as they had in Portugal. The neighborhood kids would get together after school and play sports. They would ask my brothers to play, but they wouldn't ask me because they thought I would get hurt. My brothers used to say if I couldn't play, they wouldn't play, so thanks to my brothers, I was included in these pickup games. My brothers never treated me differently; in their eyes, I was able to do just about anything, and they didn't accept anything less from me. They treated me as their equal and they didn't take any crap from me, either. If I was wrong, they would tell me about it, and sometimes we would wind up in a fistfight, the same way they handled arguments between the three of them. I usually ended up at the bottom of the pile, and they usually won the fight. But they weren't letting me off the hook, and that meant everything.

In these neighborhood games, my brothers always seemed to be on the opposite team. We would play tackle football, but when I got the ball, the kids would just tag me because they thought I was fragile. My brothers would call a time-out and say, "This is the way you do it." They would give me the ball, and then they would tackle me. Then they would look at the kids and declare, "This is the way you play football." As I remember, that was the first time I ever enjoyed pain. It felt good to be treated the same as everyone else.

8

I had the kind of personality that made friends easily when given the chance. I always had the desire to really know the people around me. For the most part, people were very nice at first, but weren't sure how to react towards me, because there were few others in Bristol with disabilities. I really think that a lot of people said hello because some of them felt empathy for me, but once they gave me a chance, they took me into their hearts. Even though they didn't have that many handicapped people in their community, they accepted me as one of their own. When I was down and out, there was always someone to pick me up, dust me off, and put me "back on my horse." At the time, Bristol was a very small community, and everybody knew each other by first name. Word got around quickly about me, and people were generally concerned for my well-being. As I look back, the people in my community really embraced me as their own son.

My parents treated me differently than my brothers did. They coddled me. I had my parents buffaloed, and it would make my brothers angry. I went from one extreme to the other. On one hand, my brothers were trying to treat me normally so I could learn how to cope with my disability, but my parents defeated their purpose by being overprotective. I guess my parents had vowed to each other to look after me, and they hadn't figured out that the best thing was to help me be as self-sufficient as possible.

I think that my parents couldn't really come to grips with the fact that they had four children and that one of them was disabled. They continued, my father especially, to try to find help to improve my condition. Even though I was walking, they wanted me to walk like everybody else did, so they kept spending a lot of money. They would take me to places like New York, Boston, and Providence to see specialists, and all with the same results. I remember my father working three jobs just to support the family and be able to afford all these doctors' visits. His main job was working at the Converse Shoes factory, but he also had two part-time jobs: painting and cleaning chicken coops. At the same time, my mother had her first job, working at the American Tourister factory, making luggage. They rarely saw each other because they worked different shifts, and they communicated by notes left on the kitchen table.

I felt guilty because I felt I was getting all the attention from the family, and I was the reason that my brothers did not get all that they needed from our parents. I always felt that my parents singled me out, and whenever my brothers needed attention, my parents would put them on the back burner. I think my brothers understood.

September came along once again, and it was back to school. Again, I looked for Billy, still with no success. Classmates from the previous year got together to talk about their vacation over the summer, and it was nice to see all of them back. It seemed that my disability disappeared when I was around them. Still, I had an empty feeling because I knew I was still alone. Even though the walls between my classmates and me were coming down, there was still one that I could never climb. I could not play sports. That would haunt me for the next few years of my life.

My grades were excellent again. Some classmates continued to come to me for extra help. I would never say no to anyone because when I was helping someone, I felt more a part of things. A lesson taught to us by our parents was one of the most important lessons I have been fortunate to learn. They always told us, "Whatever you take, you must replace," and taught us the importance of giving back. By helping others, it was a way to repay people for their friendship and acceptance. This is still pretty good advice, not just for me, but also for everyone.

Early on, I developed some philosophies that have held true for me throughout my life. Even at a young age, I realized how important people were, and when I met a new person, I always wanted to really get to know them. I learned that when you walk around with a smile, people usually will smile back. People were and still are very helpful. All you must do is ask, and most will do almost anything in their power to help you. Often, people are afraid to ask because they feel insecure or foolish. Remember, no question is ever stupid. If you don't understand something and don't ask, how are you supposed to get the answer? No matter what the circumstances are, you must ask to grow as individuals. I came to find out that school is very important to each one of us, but people and relationships are often the best teachers.

In the fifth grade, I found Billy Gordon! He finally came to the public school. Finding him was like finding my most important possession. We talked for about an hour about the good old times at Meeting Street School. One of the reasons I was glad to see him was that now I had someone who really could understand me, and I could understand him. Now I wasn't alone on one side of the fence—now I had someone to walk with at my own speed. People didn't have to wait for me, and I wouldn't have to feel bad that they WERE waiting for me. Now I really had someone I could relate to. Now I felt like a complete person, and I could be with someone who really understood my feelings. We had a lot of fun together, and whatever one of us couldn't do, the other could do—we really complemented each other. It was a good, solid relationship, where I could open up to someone besides a family member.

My parents were still trying to find out the best doctors to take care of my condition. My father would take me to any place that people would recommend. Finally, I was so frustrated from going here and going there and getting the same answer, I told my parents to please stop spending their money because I was not going to get any better. Plus, my father was still working his three jobs just to help pay for the specialists. When my brothers needed something, my parents would say no. If they held any resentment towards me, I never saw it.

9

My fifth-grade teacher, Mrs. Kaller, had a math contest. The contest was to find out who could go through the multiplication table with the fewest mistakes. I went through the entire thing without making any mistakes! My teacher never had a student do that in all her years of teaching. She didn't stop there; she also bought me a prize! School was fun at this time because everyone accepted me for who I was and I never got sick of meeting people and making friends, in fact, the more the better.

I passed to the next grade (6th), and students were starting to date. Unfortunately, the girls at that age couldn't really get comfortable with the idea of going out with a handicapped boyfriend because they didn't know how to react. That made me turn to God more: if he would heal me, maybe I could get a girlfriend. I never did get healed, but I did get some girls to go out with me. When word got around that they had a pretty good time when they went out with me, then it wasn't a problem. Still, there were a few girls who were reluctant. All in all, it wasn't a problem when word got around that I was a pretty nice guy. It seemed to me that my cerebral palsy was an added bonus.

Unfortunately, Billy didn't go with me to the sixth grade.

Instead, he went to the hospital to get an operation on his leg, and I felt I was left alone. This time, I had enough friends, and most of my classmates were very understanding.

My parents were very religious, and they made us all accompany them every Sunday at 9:30 mass. They always told me if you want to get better, you must attend church and have a lot of faith in God. I remember going with my mother to these prayer meetings, and people would pray over me. I would get disappointed because I didn't heal. I used to blame myself because I thought that maybe my faith wasn't strong enough, and that if I increased my faith, I would heal.

Frustration began to run my life. I was going to church and coming out of it the same way—disabled. I had always thought that one of these days I would surely get completely healed. That never happened. I started taking matters into my own hands. For a few weeks, I started to try to do different things. Even though I knew my body couldn't do a task, I still couldn't accept that fact, and kept trying even though I would fail. I tried day after day to carry a glass of liquid across a room, with no success. I used to walk across the room with the liquid in my hand, and before I reached my destination, the glass would be empty. I walked with a limp, and when I came down on my foot, I would spill whatever was in the glass. Even to this day, I can't carry a glass of liquid. One time, I was so frustrated that I threw the glass across the room. I believe that was the first time I felt self-pity.

I went to Junior High School, and the students started to develop their own groups and friendships. I never fit in with a particular group, so basically, I was riding the bench, a baseball term. That was hard—even though I had a lot of friends, I felt like I was an outsider looking in. I never really found my niche in school. I guess that was the beginning of my downfall. If I associated with anyone, I felt deep inside that I didn't belong, so slowly I detached myself from anyone and everybody. I started to develop my own little world, a world that only I was allowed to go in, no one else. Friends and family members were very concerned about me.

My grades also started to drop, but I really didn't care. It was a growing problem, but I thought it was everyone else's problem, not mine. I started to get into fights at school, fights that I started. If I thought that someone looked at me kind of strangely, I would walk up to them and punch them. I also started to blame everybody around me for everything that went wrong, but I wouldn't blame myself. I was never the problem.

My family life wasn't great, either. I would start fights with my own brothers. Then I would go to my parents and blame my brothers for hitting me, and they would get into trouble. I was using my handicap as a crutch, and everybody who knew me didn't like it one bit. The more I fought my family, the easier it got, so naturally I continued to do it more and more. It was about this time that I stopped caring about others. My classmates would ask for help, and I would tell them where to go, or I would make excuses and get out of it. With my changed attitude, I started to lose a lot of friends who really cared for me. Day by day, I was just pushing everyone away because I just wanted to be left alone.

I entered the seventh grade. That is where I met my guidance counselor, James Alves. He took me aside and explained to me that he would do anything in his power to make life a little easier for me. He started by introducing me to my rehabilitation counselor, a woman named Susan Olson. With her warm smile and caring attitude, she tried to get me to open myself up to her. We met once a week. She got me involved in a Vocational Rehabilitation program that met weekly, occupied my spare time, and got me involved with some handicapped agencies. As the weeks went by, I began to let my guard down and trust Susan. Deep down in my heart, she was my best friend without a doubt. She was really a special person.

Mr. Alves was keeping a close eye on my progress. No matter how busy he was, he always put his work aside and had time for me. My grades at this time were very poor, but I managed to get into high school. I really thought that when I got to high school, things would be better for me. I was in for a rude awakening because in high school, you are dealing with five different grade levels. Of course, I thought everyone would be catering to me, but I couldn't be further from the truth.

Academically, I started out well, and I was motivated because in high school, you have to maintain good grades in order to play sports. When the signup sheet came out, I would always put my name up there. I believe that year, I signed up for three different kinds of sports: football, baseball, and wrestling. When I found out I could not play because of my cerebral palsy, even though my grades were good, I was crushed, but I did not give up.

I tried to convince the coaches to let me play, and I even suggested that I could play on special teams on the football team. The coaches didn't share the same opinion as I did, and because they were afraid that I might get hurt, they said no. The hopes that I had going into high school disappeared. I think that was the first time that I became very bitter. My insides became like vinegar. I was a young man getting out of control with my environment, as well as my emotions, so I shut down and blocked everyone out.

Anything that went wrong, I would say, "Don't blame me, blame my Cerebral Palsy." My grades were no longer improving, and I did not care. My classmates would ask me for help, and I would tell them that I was too busy and then blow them off. I was angry with my Cerebral Palsy, yet I used it to distance myself from others. I fought with friends, family, teachers, and helpers.

That was the year that I finally came to the realization that I wasn't going to get any better. My faith in God healing my body was gone. In fact, I said, "God, when I die, and I am standing before you at 'Judgment Day,' you are going to answer me and tell me why I was born this way." At this point, I felt that it wasn't fair that everyone around me was physically able, and I was not. I really wanted someone to give me an explanation, and no one could answer this question: "Why did God make me become disabled without a fighting chance?" I decided then to only have faith in myself, no longer God, and to take control of my life.

10

I was struggling emotionally, spiritually, and mentally, not to mention physically!

Even though I struggled, people kept showing up in my life. Three of my friends who looked after me in different ways were Richard "Richie," who owns a construction company, and two police officers named Thomas and John. People like them tried to really help me to cope with my situation, and surprisingly enough, sometimes I listened to them.

Richie was and still is one of the wealthiest men in Bristol, RI. He took a liking to me and always told me to be patient and that everything would fall into place. Our friendship grew in leaps and bounds. He treated me like his own son, and no matter where I went, I did not have to worry about paying for anything. Richie knew my family's financial situation and that my father was still working three jobs. I felt bad that he always paid for things, but he told me, "Joe, I like you and I see a lot in you, so whatever I do, please accept."

Richie sponsored a softball team, and he knew how much I liked sports, so he made me his third base coach. I remember once he got a double. The next person got a single, and I waved Richie home, but he stopped at third base. Later, I asked him, "Hey Richie, how come you didn't score on that single?" He replied, "Joe, because you shake, I wasn't sure if you were telling me to go home or stop at third!" That was the first time I ever laughed at myself, especially the way he was telling that story to the rest of the teammates.

After that incident at third base, they moved me over to coach first base, thinking I could be more effective there. But one day, I got my wish.... I got to play. We were playing a team from Costa's Fruitland. We were short a guy because some people had not shown up. Rather than forfeit, they put me in right field, because as Richie said, "No one ever hits to right field." Well, wouldn't you know it? A ball got hit to right field. I ran further and further back, trying to catch the ball. I got to the point where I could not go back any farther. Finally, someone yelled, "Joe, where are you going?" I said, "I'm going after the ball!" They said, "The ball's over here!" Then I realized I had been trying to catch a bird. With the sun in my eyes, it looked white, and I thought it was the ball. I got a lot of ribbing over that!

Another time, we were playing a team from Micheletti's Restaurant. They put me in with the score tied and the bases loaded. Somehow, I got lucky...the opposing pitcher walked me. All I had to do was walk to first base and touch the bag. The walk moved the runners around and forced in the winning run, and I did not even get a hit! These are just some examples of how Richie was one of many important people in my life.

Susan, my rehab counselor, continued to be especially important to me. I was always interested in what she had to say. She told me, "Since you like sports so much, why don't you join the Special Olympics?" I agreed and I signed up for everything that I could. I used to practice every day on my own, getting ready for a competition. That year, we went to Springfield, MA, for the regional competition. I was in four events—weightlifting, archery, wrestling, and indoor soccer. With my attitude the way it was, I thought I was going to win my events with the greatest of ease—I was totally wrong.

My first event was indoor soccer, and when I saw everybody in wheelchairs, I said to myself, "This is going to be a cakewalk," because I was the only one who could walk. Then they told me to get into my wheelchair. I was stunned! I got into my wheelchair, and I could not move in the direction that I wanted to go! Everyone was going up and down the court, and I had great difficulty just maneuvering my wheelchair. I got so frustrated that I got up from my wheelchair and drew a penalty. We won the game, surprisingly by one point..

After the game, I went up to one of my teammates and asked why I had trouble maneuvering my wheelchair. Rather than just showing me the mechanics of a wheelchair, he told me that the experience of it not being easy for me is exactly what the doctor had ordered. He explained, "You are a very competitive young man, and just maybe this experience will make you realize how fortunate you are." He looked at me and said, "If you think you have it bad, just look at these players out here on the court today. Watch who can or cannot get up from their wheelchair anytime they want. I did watch and noticed that I was one of the only ones who had been able to learn to walk. This helped me start to realize that I was luckier than I had thought.

The Special Olympics was a great outlet, but I felt unsatisfied because it was not a replacement for what I considered real sports, so I dropped out of it. I continued to search for where I fit, but I could not find the answer that I was looking for. Deep down in my heart, I had my answer; however, I just did not like it. I just could not accept the fact that I was disabled. This dilemma continued to taunt me.

Sometimes it feels like I have two people living in one body. My brain tells my body to do a particular task, and my body tells my brain that I cannot do it. That is where the battle begins with my brain versus my body. Ironically, neither of them could ever win, so I wish that one of them would simply give up—that way I could live a physically normal life; however, rather than leaving me stuck in the middle.

11

By this time, Ms. Olsen and I had become very good friends. I was opening up to her and sharing some of my deep inner feelings. I was still very bitter towards the world in general. I could not accept the fact that everybody walked better than I did and functioned better than I did. Susan would show me how to compensate, and I would simply tell her, "If I can't do it right, I won't do it at all." Again, with that attitude, I was not getting anywhere fast.

My grades at that time were barely passable and on the verge of failing. I think by the eighth grade, I stopped doing homework, never studied, and when it was time for exams, I used to cram all night. I really did not care because I felt I had been cheated and robbed of the life I should have had, and nothing mattered, especially at that age. All that I was concerned with was being physically normal so I could play sports.

Somehow, my grades were good enough so that I passed into the ninth grade, but they were not as good as they had previously been. Before, I was getting A's and B's; now I was getting C's, D's, and a few F's. I was messed up, and it continued into the ninth grade. The ninth grade was interesting because all the students started to have long-term relationships and friendships, but because of my attitude, I never established those kinds of relationships. Most of my friends left me because I drove them away. I really started to dislike everybody around me, and when people tried to get closer to me, I thought they were doing it out of pity.

I entered the ninth grade with the same students from the previous year; different teachers, of course, different studies, but the same crummy attitude. My mantra that year was "do to them before they do unto you." With that way of thinking... well, I really was not going to make many friends, was I? I started to get into more fights—about two fights every week. I always got called down to the principal's office. He was nice and tried to be understanding to me, but would always say, "Joe, I like you a lot, but every time you come down into my office, you tie my hands." That really did not stop me—I continued to do whatever I pleased, and no one could tell me different.

I was three years older than my classmates, so I hung around with a crowd that was much older than the kids who were in my classes. I made a lot of friends outside of school. The reason I was three years older than my classmates was that when I came from São Miguel, Azores, and did not know the English language, they put me in special education classes to learn the language. My classmates and I really did not have that much in common outside of school, so basically, I hung around with people around my age when school was not in session.

My relationships at home were not getting any better either. I used to resent my brothers simply because everything they did of a physical nature was easy for them. I would struggle just to do anything physically. I was really going on the wrong path with no relief in sight. My parents—well, I had them in my hip pocket, and I could do anything to them whenever I desired. They were like my puppets, and all I had to do was pull strings.

I started to experiment with alcohol, drinking here and there, but never getting really drunk. However, it made me really relaxed, and that is one thing I had never really experienced. Without anything in my system, I could not carry liquid in my hands and walk at the same time. However, when I had alcohol in my system…Well, I could do that and a whole lot more. I could not wait to get out of school so I could buy a six-pack of Miller beer. I just wanted to escape the world that I was in and create my own little universe. Alcohol gave me a world that only existed when I drank, plus, I could pick the people that I wanted to share it with.

Slowly, I began to withdraw from everyone and everything around me. If I could not do a particular task, I wouldn't bother anyone to help me; I just wanted to be left alone. I know now that pride can destroy a person internally without that person even knowing. At that time, I had too much pride, and it was destroying me. A personality that people had envied and admired was disappearing, and I did not care.

The coaches who ran the sports department in school tried very hard to get me involved. They knew I had the desire to play, but I could not, so they tried to make me an assistant. I loved playing sports so much that I quit being an assistant. The problem escalated because I envisioned myself playing professionally someday.

When I entered the eleventh grade, the Head Counselor called me in. His name was Joseph Caromile, another wonderful person. He asked me what my plans were after high school, and I told him I simply did not care. He asked me if I wanted to go to college. I told him that I had never given that any consideration, and if I had problems in high school, then I would have even more problems in college. My grades were not good enough to attend any college anyway, so I said no. Besides, all I wanted to do was just to take everything day by day; I really did not have any vision or plan for my future. All I knew was that I did not want to be disabled, and I was still bitter and angry.

I continued to drink at a steady clip, and now I was getting drunk at least four to five times a week. I was simply at a point where I was out of control. The Catholic morals and values that my parents taught me throughout my life were gone. I simply did not have anything to live by; I just did whatever I pleased, and no one, including my parents, could ever tell me what to do.

School was going awful—teachers wanted to help me improve my grades, but I refused their help. I believed that the school would hand me my diploma because I was disabled, even if I failed out! So, I continued to meet my friends after school, and we would drink all afternoon. I would come home drunk. My parents would ask where I had been, and I would say I was with my friends.

It was not fun getting drunk; however, drinking made me more relaxed, and the more I drank, the steadier I was. Getting drunk was a negative way to cope with my disability. Being a teenager was tough enough, and drinking relieved my frustrations. Drinking made me feel equal to my peers. When I was not drinking, all I thought about was my disability, and I couldn't stand that. I could not accept it, and I wasn't going to accept it. My brothers were still around, trying to help me. They told me to stop drinking, but I did not want to listen. It was the one time that I felt physically normal, and I did not want to let that go.

12

My classmates tried to help me cope with my disability, and they showed sincerity; however, I used to tell them, "Unless you are in my shoes, you can never understand what I'm going through." I would never wish the pain that I was going through on anybody else. Loneliness is something no one should experience in their lifetime. Even though I had people around me, I was an arm's length away from them. Subconsciously, I wanted to break down the barriers; consciously, I would not allow myself to get into that position and experience any more of that hurt.

A pivotal problem that I continued to have was that I could not play any kind of sports in school. I could not accept it because all I wanted to do was to play. One day I went to a football game—I went in by myself, and I sat away from everybody. I started to cry because I wanted to be on that field. I closed my eyes and played the game in my mind. When reality set in that I still had cerebral palsy, a new rage started to build within me.

My brother Thomas, who was a good student, was always home doing his homework. For some reason, Thomas and I were extremely competitive. We always tried to outdo each other—out of the three brothers, he was the only one I used to enjoy getting into a dispute with. I used to come into the house drunk and get into an argument with him. Now, Thomas did not drink—in fact, he disliked anyone who really got drunk. Since I always used to be drunk almost every day, my relationship with him was not the greatest. Every time I came in, I always started to argue with him, and we would wind up in a fistfight. Of course, my parents believed that I had never started anything, so when my parents found out what happened, my brother would get in trouble, and I got off scot-free.

I continued my weekly visits to the principal's office because of the fighting. As I was leaving his office one day, he said something very interesting to me. He looked at me, put his arm around my shoulders, and said, "When are you going to bring the other side of yourself back, because you aren't realizing the kind of inspiration that you bring to others?" I thought he was crazy, because how can a handicap inspire people?

I continued to drink just to escape reality—I just could not face it anymore. I started coming to school with a big hangover from the previous night. My grades were slipping downward to the point where I could not control them. Classmates asked me to study with them, but I would not hear of it. All I wanted to do was to drink and get drunk just to escape the pain, the pain that I created for myself. I thought that I was so far away from everybody that I could not reach out to anyone and open up to them. I kept on hoping that the roller coaster would just stop and let me off.

I had started drinking a shot or two of liquor in the mornings in eleventh grade. The alcohol relaxed me enough that I could carry a glass of liquid and did not have all the spasms that I usually had. By twelfth grade, I was drinking even more in the mornings. I was coming to school drunk. The head of the language department, Mr. Almedia, stopped me one day because he could smell the alcohol on my breath. He told me that I had better stop before something serious happened. But I did not listen.

I started skipping days from school, because I was so hungover that I could not get up, and I couldn't face the fact of being disabled anymore. I kept to myself mostly; when someone approached me and said, "How are you doing?" I would say "fine," when in reality I wanted to open up to someone and tell them the truth, but that word "pride" kept me from being able to do that. I wanted someone to sit me down and explain to me why I was born with cerebral palsy.

If I had been paying attention, I would have seen that there were signs telling me to get my life in order. Mr. Caromile called me in and said, "Joe, I have bad news for you. You will not graduate with your class." I looked at him and laughed and told him that the school was going to let me graduate because I was disabled. At that point, he shut the door to his office and said, "When are you going to stop using your handicap as a crutch?" I looked at him and started crying, and told him that the school would not let me play sports. He looked at me and said, "Joe, would you believe when I was your age, I was too short to play football at the time? So, they did not let me play either." I looked at him and told him, "At least you had the chance and gave it your best shot, but I never had the chance to at least get cut from the team."

I left school that day feeling so depressed that I bought two six packs of beer and proceeded to drink. I tried to put my life into perspective, but I could not because I thought I didn't have anything to build on. I started to feel sorry for myself because I really could not comprehend at that point in time, because I was born with cerebral palsy, and everyone else was born physically normal. I always had a vivid imagination, and drinking made it more vivid, and I could imagine anything when I was drunk.

That night, I was completely drunk, and I saw my brother studying, and I argued with him again. As I mentioned, my brother Thomas was always studying and getting good grades. He looked at me and said, "Joe, when you are drunk, I don't even want to know you. You think that everything comes easy for me—well, you are wrong, I must study to get good grades. Do not think that the world owes something to you because it doesn't." Michael and Victor walked in together and joined the conversation. My brothers sat me down and tried to drill it into my head that when you cannot solve the problem, you must work around it. Finally, they all agreed that no one wanted to hurt me, but I was hurting myself and the people who loved me. Even though I did not want to hear it, they were right.

Deep down in my heart, I always knew that I was not going to strike out. Deep down in my heart, there was a better tomorrow. One thing I am incredibly grateful for is that I never thought of suicide, because if I did, I believe that I wouldn't be here today.

I finally started to get the message. I went home that evening drunk as usual. I went to my room, got undressed, knelt near my bed, and said, "God, if you are real, please help me because I am not doing a very good job." I poured out my heart, hoping that someone or something would just sweep me off my feet. That night, I cried myself to sleep, but I made a deal with God. I simply told Him that if He would change my life, I would try to help everybody who crossed my path.

The next morning, I didn't think much about the previous night, but I did get up with a different attitude, an attitude that I used to know in the past. I also noticed something different in the mirror. The person I was looking at was a nice guy and had a nice smile. I did the same thing that I always did during the school day, but with a different attitude. After school, I went to the liquor store and bought a six-pack, went to my favorite spot, and started to drink. I always noticed that after drinking three beers, I would be getting drunk, so I went ahead and drank the other three in the six-pack. I was perplexed because I had just drank six beers, and I was not drunk. I thought the beer was just flat and did not contain alcohol. I got home and saw my brother Thomas studying. Automatically, he thought I was going to start with him, but to his surprise, I asked him, "How was your day?" He looked at me kind of confused and answered, "Fine."

When my other brothers got home, I asked them, "OK, guys, what are we doing today?" My brother Michael looked at me and said, "Joe, are you feeling alright?" All of them were used to me wanting to be left alone and do my own thing. When they noticed my attitude had changed, they thought that I wanted to manipulate them, but all that I wanted was to be with them. Deep down in my heart, I knew I hurt each one of them. Even my parents asked me what was wrong. I just could not explain it or figure it out, and I wasn't going to try; I just was going to ride it out as long as it lasted.

I went to school the next morning, and I saw students I had tried to avoid, and now I approached them, asking them how they were doing. I thought something was wrong with me because my attitude changed for the better, and I couldn't understand why or how. Instead of avoiding people, now I was approaching them. My teachers were amazed by my different outlook. For example, instead of covering up for my disability, now I was talking about it. I could not hide it, so why not start to use it as an asset? The moment I tried to accept it, the better and easier things got for me, and the more I realized that my disability was not a crutch anymore; instead, it was a gem in the rough.

If any of you lacks wisdom, you should ask God, who gives generously to all without finding fault, and it will be given to you. But when you ask, you must believe and not doubt, because the one who doubts is like a wave of the sea, blown and tossed by the wind. James 1:5-6, NIV.

Mr. Caromile called me into his office again and told me again, "Joe, you are not going to be graduating with your class, because there is no way that you can make up all these credits." Out of the 180 days that made up a school year, I had missed one hundred. Even though my grades were good enough that I could have passed twelfth grade, I had not been in the classroom enough days to get credit for attendance as required by the state. Now my reaction was different, and I took responsibility for my actions. Of course, I was upset at myself and myself only, but I looked at him and said, "All right, not this year, but I will graduate next year."

When I got home, my brother Thomas was there, and he saw me upset. He tried to comfort me as I told him why I was upset. I simply told him, "Thomas, it's nobody's fault but my own." I believe that at that moment, I matured and understood, at once, that whatever you do in life, you have to do it with the best of your ability. The only regret that I had was that I wished that I could change some parts of my past, but that was impossible.

13

I went to see Mr. Caromile again, and I told him I was interested in going to college. He looked at me and smiled and said, "You don't know how long I've been waiting to hear those words come out of your mouth!" I wanted to go to Johnson & Wales College (now University) and study Business Management, but Mr. Caromile did not think they would accept me because of my grades. However, he said, I had a year to bring up my grades and prove to the college that they should take a risk and at least accept me on a trial basis.

My brother Thomas was ready to graduate. He came up to me and said, "Joe, I wish you were up there with me." I told him that it was my own fault, and besides, it was his time to shine, and he deserved it. I told him, "I may not be there physically, but I will be there in spirit." It would have been nice if I could have graduated with my brother; however, that was not to be.

The summer that followed, Camp Stone Tower was looking for volunteers. Camp Stone Tower is a summer camp for mentally challenged campers. My summer was free, so I volunteered. When we think that we do not have anything to offer, we must think again. There are always people out there who are in greater need than you and really could use you in some capacity. I did not know it at the time, but this was one of the greatest experiences in my life because I finally moved my focus from myself to someone else. At the beginning of the summer, I had thought that, being disabled, I could not do much. That was the way that I felt. However, Camp Stone Tower helped me change that attitude, especially when I found out that they needed my help, and I learned that I could be a positive role model to the campers.

In life, there are no accidents. Camp Stone Tower came into my life at a time when I was open and ready to receive God's hand in my life. I did not know it then, but I see now that once I lowered my walls and let God (and other people) in, I was able to see that there was more to my life than I had thought. I was able to step outside myself and focus on someone else. By helping these folks, as I had promised, I felt like I was useful and had a purpose. God does work in mysterious ways; all we must do is ask for help.

I came out of my shell that summer because I began to accept that I was not going to get better physically. Once I did that, I put everything else into better perspective. And I began to realize that no matter where I would go, people would stop and notice me; so, my attitude had to be right, because if my attitude was not right, then my testimony wouldn't have any value. If there was one thing I had to work on, it was my attitude, because even though I was more accepting of my disability, still, at times, if I was not on guard, the negativity would hit hard.

That summer, I met another wonderful man by the name of Manuel Pimental. He was working at the United Cerebral Palsy Chapter of Rhode Island as a fundraiser. I called him and we met, and we had instant respect for each other. He wanted me to help him in fundraising activities, but I told him that I could not do much because of my commitment to Camp Stone Tower and school. He simply told me, "Whatever you do, it would be a bonus." Manuel continued to invite me to help him out, and I relented and committed myself to him and the United Cerebral Palsy organization. He and I worked on several different kinds of fundraisers. I really enjoyed what I was doing, and I was getting to know people who really enjoyed what they were doing. Meeting other people with cerebral palsy also made it easier to cope with this condition. I was even asked to speak to parents about cerebral palsy.

Throughout my life, a lot of people saw the potential that I had, but I could not see it. As far as I was concerned, I was not anyone special. Parents used to come to me and say, "Thanks to you, I am able to understand my child better," and "Thanks to you, I am able to let go of some of the fears that I have about tomorrow." I used to go home perplexed because I was not sure what I was doing that was so special; however, it was a good feeling, and I wasn't going to stop whatever I was doing.

September rolled around, and it was time to go back to school and time to enter the twelfth grade once again, but this time I was determined to complete it with flying colors. When I opened the door to the school, the first face I saw was Mr. Caromile. He looked at me and said, "This is the year!" I responded by saying, "I may stay back once more just to give you more gray hairs!" He said, "If you stay back again, I will personally throw you out with my foot!" That is how I got the message that he wanted me to graduate!

I really wanted to do well, not only to graduate but also to go to college, so I had to get on the ball. I studied extremely hard, and my grades were above average. My friends and I used to study together, and I did everything that I could to do my best. I really worked hard in my second senior year in high school, and I tried to make amends for the past. Someone told me to forget the past and live in the present, but deep down in my heart, I knew I had hurt so many people, and I prayed that someday they would forgive me. I also knew that I could not bring the past back, and if they were my real friends, they would forgive me.

In April, I applied to Johnson & Wales. They were very pleasant and arranged a tour for me, showing me the campus. Finally, they talked to me about what they expected out of me. In return, they promised a good education. They told me they would evaluate my application and get back to me within the next two months.

Two months went by, and I received a letter from Johnson & Wales. I was so afraid of being rejected that I could not even open it. After being rejected for so many years, I thought one more time should not bother me, but still, I couldn't open it. That night, I could not sleep; I tossed and turned. The next morning, the letter was staring me in the face. I took it to school and gave it to Mr. Caromile and asked him to open it. He opened it, looked at me, smiled, and offered his congratulations. There was a condition in the letter, which stated that I was accepted only on a trial basis. I really did not care because all my life it seemed like I was always on some type of trial, so why should this be any different?

The rest of the school year went fine. I maintained good grades and was ready to go forward and continue my education. I made sure to enjoy my senior year as much as I could by getting involved in my class's activities. When it came to sports, I did not attend. Deep down in my heart, I wanted to be out there more than anything else at that time; more than life itself. Some of my closest friends knew what I was going through, and they tried extremely hard to comfort me. I did appreciate their help, but there was nothing that they could do. I had to go through it by myself. Sometimes I used to dwell on my inability to play sports too much, but I could not afford to dwell on negative things. I had too much to lose.

Graduation was the end of the school year, and it would be the end of a chapter. I was emotional because I knew I would leave an impact on the high school. I became sad when I thought that it could be negative! I was twenty-one years old. I made it, and it was time to enjoy it along with my classmates. I got fitted for my cap and gown and then enjoyed Senior Week to the fullest with the class of 1980! I received my yearbook, and to my surprise, so many people, even those that I did not know, signed my yearbook. I was worried about leaving behind negative, but my classmates were making sure that I left school feeling that I was leaving behind positive!

I went to rehearsal for the graduation ceremony, and suddenly it hit me like a lightning bolt that what I was about to accomplish was something beyond my wildest dreams. I finally did it!! Now I was ready to accept my diploma with honor and self-assurance. I also knew that no one could ever take this accomplishment away from me.

On June 19, 1980, my class and I went on stage to get what we had worked so hard for. My whole family was in attendance that evening, and I was extremely excited. When my name was called and I went to accept my diploma, my class stood up and gave me a standing ovation. Then the audience got up and joined in the ovation. That ovation lasted about ten minutes, and it felt like it would not stop. I looked at my family, showed them my diploma, and thanked them. I never expected that kind of acclaim. My classmates were acknowledging all the struggles I had been through, and that I had turned my life around. That was the nicest thing they could ever have done for me.

14

There was a beautiful young lady I liked very much in high school. Every time that I passed by her and gazed into her beautiful green eyes, something inside of me moved. It was a great feeling. Catherine was her name. She was a respected, intelligent, polite, kind, sincere, and beautiful young lady who always had a kind word for everyone. Days went by, and every time I saw her, warm feelings welled up inside me, feelings that I had never experienced. In high school, among her peers, she never judged anyone. I really had taken a liking to Catherine and those beautiful green eyes. I would go out of my way just to run into her, and I would walk her to class and then run to my class. I was always late for my class because I couldn't run like other students. My teachers were very forgiving when I was late. Catherine was a knockout. She was everything that a teenage boy could crush on in high school. She was shy and blushed very easily. We became good friends over time, and I always put her on top of a pedestal in my heart. Everyone has a crush on someone, and Catherine was mine; she was the young lady that I had been waiting for. I never asked her out because I was always keenly aware of my physical limitations, and never thought very highly of myself in high school because of these limitations. How could I care for someone else when I did not care for myself?

It was a rainy, raw day in school when Catherine walked by me to say hello. We talked for a couple of minutes between classes. Five minutes into class, the sun came out, and there was a rainbow. I just closed my eyes and said to myself, "Catherine, you are my pot of gold." I was truly blessed to know a wonderful, caring, and beautiful classmate named Catherine. She was always willing to help others. The real beauty about her was inside of her, that wonderful spirit of gentleness and a big heart to have the ability to touch people just with her words. She was fun to be around, and I really enjoyed being in her presence.

I never liked clicks in school, and she wasn't into any of that. Let me tell you, Catherine should have been the homecoming queen every year. I know it does not work like that, but all around, she is the best lady with none of the other young ladies in high school coming even close to her. In my opinion, she was the only one who mattered. She was a very humble person and never dramatic. To me, she didn't belong in this era. She reminded me of this maiden who is always willing to help in any way that she can. When I was with her, she made me feel like a person with meaning.

Catherine always impressed me as someone genuine, never a phony, and she never had a hard word to say about anyone. There was always a smile on that beautiful face, and she brought sunshine no matter where she went. I was honored and privileged to know such a wonderful person. Catherine touched my heart like no one in high school. Unfortunately, I couldn't take the next step and tell her my feelings and ask her out. That's okay because I truly know what a friend really means, and her name is Catherine. She is pure sunshine.

Part Two

15

The following summer, I worked awfully hard as a fundraiser for United Cerebral Palsy. I also realized that my personality was one of the best tools that I could have to be successful. I raised quite a bit of money for the organization. I felt proud to help in any way that I could.

Also, that summer, I worked with the mentally disadvantaged population again at Camp Stone Tower and found that the more time that I gave them, the more blessings I received. I learned that when you stop focusing on yourself and focus on others who are in need, you can make a world of difference. A person will never realize what he or she has until they share it with others who do not have it. When you share the talent that you have with someone who is less fortunate than you are, then you experience the wonder of sharing and giving. I totally believe in the laws of giving: the more you give, the more you receive. There is something within us that, when we give, there is a certain kind of peace, a peace not fully understood. The more you do it, the better person you are towards your fellow man. When we stop dwelling on our own problems and help others with theirs, our problems start to seem smaller.

September came along, and that meant college was ready to begin. I was skeptical because deep down in my heart, I did not want to be there, because I often wondered how I was going to compete with everyone there. It was a tough adjustment, but deep down, I knew that if I was going to compete with the people in the world, then I had to compete with the students at college.

College was tough in the beginning because I believed that for every step that a student took, I had to take two, and every two they took, I had to take four, but I kept up with my fellow students. Everyone there was also helpful, whatever I lacked; the students were there to help me carry on.

Johnson & Wales College was set up by trimester, which meant every twelve weeks we changed classes. I did quite well in the first trimester. Johnson & Wales College was in the city, which meant they had buildings all over the city, and the students had ten minutes to get from class to class. I was always late, of course, but the professors understood the situation. In high school, I always hung around with friends and family, and I spent a lot of time inside. I never paid that much attention to the snowfall in the winter; however, in college, there was a significant difference because I had to do so much walking. When the snow came, I tried to walk to my classes and could not because I used to fall and crack my head against the concrete, and blood used to rush down my head, and then I would not go to class because I had to go back to my room at school and change up. By the time I had caught my breath and was ready to go to class, it was over.. Since Johnson & Wales was a business school, it had a business policy that stated if a student was absent more than three times, then he or she would automatically fail the course.

My grades dropped dramatically, and I tried to attend classes, but I could not. The students tried to walk with me and carry my books, and it worked for a while; however, it was making them late, too. Finally, I told them to go ahead and that

I would get there eventually. Of course, I did not. I remembered one time I took a bad fall and I really hurt myself. I got down on my knees and said, "Lord, I worked so hard to get where I am, why am I going through this?"

I met a student by the name of Donna. We became particularly good friends. We did everything together, and we enjoyed each other's company, whether studying or just going for a cup of coffee. She was my best friend in college. Donna tried to help me cope with my disability, but that did not work. She was physically able, and naturally, I have cerebral palsy. This difference got into my head and bothered me.

I see now that when we concentrate on ourselves and pick at the negative things in our lives, we can drag ourselves down until we start to concentrate on the positive things.

In fact, I believe that I drove her away. When we were together, I tried to analyze our relationship. I could not justify it because I felt that she deserved better than me, at least physically. Every time we got together, I would purposely start a disagreement, but she was patient and saw my own internal struggles, and she put up with it for a while. Our friendship was falling apart, and the cause of it was my own because I kept testing her. I started to put her in situations that she did not want to be in.

I looked at her one day and asked why she was with me. She told me, "If you don't know by now, you will never know." She was pretty fed up with me, and said, "Joe, I would like to thank you from the bottom of my heart for making my mind up for me. You are not the same person that I once knew."

Back in my mind, I thought that everything after high school would fall into place. Getting through more than twelve years of school had a silver lining—college. I guess the things that I wanted the most were impossible—physical agility. Now it was up to me to really decide on realistic things that I knew I could achieve. But that was not good enough for me. Deep down in my heart, I had to prove myself to the people around me.

At the time, the Dean of Johnson & Wales academics was a man by the name of Dr. Koch. He called me into his office and told me that I was in danger of not making the grades. He realized my potential and understood the dilemma that I was facing. He suggested that I should consider attending night school. After thoughtful consideration, I agreed, because I knew how much I had overcome through the years, and I didn't want to quit now.

I finished that trimester in the day program. Once the new trimester started, I went into the evening division. I took two courses per week. Each class lasted four hours. I really did not mind because at least I wasn't walking long distances from class to class. The students there were of various ages, and I really enjoyed that very much, because I got to relate to points of view from different age groups. My grade point average while taking evening classes was a little better than a 3.00 average, which comes out to a B average. I was pleased with myself, not only with my grades, but I believe for the first time in my heart, I finally came to the realization that I could keep up with my fellow students. That was another turning point in my life.

16

I wanted to take a couple of courses over the summer, but I was advised to take the summer off. Unfortunately, I could not find a summer job, so I did volunteer work with United Cerebral Palsy by helping them with fundraising. I really enjoyed it because I enjoy meeting people. Plus, I was extremely outgoing and was more than willing to try almost anything to raise money. I knew that I really did not have any limitations in that area.

One person who really inspired me over the years was Jerry Lewis and the Muscular Dystrophy Association (MDA) telethon. He was a man who had everything that he could ever want and need, yet he still dedicated his time to help the MDA. Jerry Lewis really made an impression on my heart. If he could inspire me and reach millions of people, then I felt that I should do my part, whether big or small. I really enjoyed his telethon for two reasons: one, it impressed me in my heart how really blessed I was, and two, it showed me different ways to raise money.

September came along again, and that meant back to school and study. But this time I had an incentive—come May, I would get my Associate's Degree. I studied hard plus attended various functions and fundraising activities. I had a very trying schedule, but I enjoyed it. What I enjoyed most was meeting people from all different walks of life. People from the United Cerebral Palsy wanted me to give talks to parents with children with cerebral palsy. Initially, I felt I was not the right candidate because I was still sorting out my own personal problems. On the other hand, I felt honored because if they asked me, it meant I had to be doing something right, so I agreed to do it. Plus, Manny Pimental threatened that if I didn't do it, he would make me "walk straight." I never knew what that meant, but for the same reason, I am glad I never found out!

Once you start to talk about certain situations in your life, then they become easier to deal with, and people were extremely interested in what I had to say. And once I started to talk about myself, living with this disability, I finally understood what my life was all about. I slowly began to accept my disability. If I had a choice, naturally, I would want to have normal physical ability. By the same token, I started to realize that without this disability, I might not be the person that I was becoming. Having cerebral palsy made me the best person that I can be.

The month of May came along, and I finally graduated. I did not attend graduation because my intention was to start right away on my job search. Unfortunately, when you think you have an upper hand on life, then, for some reason without explanation, life deals you a different hand. I had my Associate's Degree, and I really believed that I would get through an employer's door. My resume looked surprisingly good, but I kept getting the standard rejection letter. By this point, I was starting to get frustrated with companies.

I did get a telephone call from a company to come in and fill out the application. When my interviewer came and asked for Joseph Ferreira, naturally, I stood up. He was shocked because he looked at my resume and looked at me, and from his expression, he seemed like he had just met two different people. One he was reading about, and the other was standing before him. He gathered himself enough to give me the interview, but I declined because I sensed a lot of tension between us. I felt deep down in my heart that he would give me a fifteen-minute interview, and then I would get the standard letter. Instead of that happening I looked at him and said "Mr. so and so (his name was not important) as much as I want a job, I feel like I don't have a chance to get this job. You already gave me two strikes and I have too much pride to strike out" and I just walked away. After I told him this, I felt like I just won the lottery.

I could not find a paying job, so I started to volunteer, figuring if something came up, I would be right there and turn the volunteering into a paying job, but that never worked out either. I was getting depressed about myself. Then my luck changed! That same year, the government came out with incentives to hire handicapped individuals. The plan was that if any company hired a disabled worker, then that company would get a tax break at the end of the year. I was hired right away and was very productive, but at the end of that year, I was laid off. I came to find out that the biggest tax break was during the first year.

This happened to me a couple of times. Overall, it was a good plan, but I think that instead of the government decreasing the tax break, they should have increased it annually. Then maybe the companies would hold onto the handicapped employees longer and train them according to their abilities. I really do not blame the companies because in business, you are supposed to maximize profit and minimize cost. As soon as the federal funds ran out, the program was dropped.

At this time, I was totally frustrated, but I would not give up. My parents and my brothers would console me and comfort me, but it was still a lonely feeling, because deep down I knew I was capable, and I did not get a chance to prove it, which hurt me the most. My wonderful mother knew the trouble that I had in my life, and she also knew the struggles that I was going through. She always gave me words of encouragement. She and my father did everything for me. When I got up in the morning, they made my bed, prepared my breakfast, and washed and pressed my clothes. This bothered me because even though they deny it even to this day, they still felt responsible for my disability. For consolation, they did everything for me. I was really spoiled, and I was getting used to it.

I started to think, "If I do not ever get married, will I be able to take care of myself?" or "Will I be a burden to one of my brothers if my parents ever pass away?" As much as I love Michael, Thomas, and Victor, I do not think it would be proper to impose on them because they also have their own lives to live instead of worrying about their older brother, Joseph. And my pride would not allow that to happen.

I knew a couple in California, and we kept in touch constantly. We talked about me taking a vacation to California and staying with them, and enjoying the wonderful weather. One Christmas, they came to Rhode Island to spend the holiday season with family. They came over to my house and spent a couple of hours with me. As a Christmas gift, they gave me a ticket to go out there to visit. My parents were a little apprehensive, especially my mother. Even though I was the oldest, to my mother, I was the baby. I think she felt that way because of my disability. Even to this day, she denies it, but I knew better. I tried to convince her that this was a great opportunity for me to develop my life for the better. They finally agreed with a bit of fear.

17

On January 3, 1985, my brother Thomas drove me to the airport, and off I went to California. That drive to the airport took about an hour and a half. Even though my brother and I loved each other very much, we had a bit of a rivalry between us. We tried very hard to express ourselves, and struggled. Even though I knew what we wanted to say and vice versa. When he told me he was very proud of me, I was stunned. It brought tears to my eyes because if there was anyone in the family I had a constant battle with, it was he. I felt everything came easily to him. I was so wrong because he worked very hard for everything. But at that time, I could not see that. What it came down to was that I was still a little envious.

Thomas asked me, "How did you survive how badly Dad treated us? We brothers did not have Cerebral Palsy like you do." Thomas's words stunned me. We had never talked about this so candidly together. We always felt we should keep our father on a pedestal because of how hard he worked for us. We had kept our feelings to ourselves. In fact, our silence about our dad's treatment created division between us brothers.

In St. Miguel, Azores, my grandparents had it tough. My grandfather could not find work, so he decided to go to

Argentina. He was there for three or four months when he became ill and was paralyzed from the waist down. My grandmother became head of the household in a Patriarchal culture, but not by her choice. Being a father and a mother was no easy task for her. She expected all of her children to help out and not make mistakes. If her kids did not help her, she beat them.

One day, their oldest son, John, who worked on a fishing boat to earn money to support the family, decided to go and fish from the dock. It was terrible weather, and my grandmother begged him not to go. He told her that whatever he caught would be pure profit for the family since he did not have to share it with the boat captain. Sadly, my grandmother believed that the waves and wind from the severe weather washed him off the dock when his body washed up onto shore a few weeks later. After he died, my grandmother grew heavily dependent on my father, because he had then become the oldest of her remaining children. My father helped my grandmother with everything, but he also took responsibility for all of the family's struggles.

The following instances stick out in my mind, so I am going to share the years that they happened:

1969

When it came to religion, my father was strict. I often wondered how he could revere God. Especially considering how he treated us all. To this day, I still remember my father praying around the bed with all four boys learning our prayers. My father at the time worked the second shift (3:00 p.m. to 11:00 p.m.). One hour before he went to work, the four of us were on our knees learning our prayers. If I messed up, he would hit me with the belt.

Friends of my parents went to St. Miguel, Azores, on

vacation. This was my parents' old hometown. Two weeks later, they came back and brought my parents a gift. It was a pair of beautiful candlesticks. My father put the candlesticks in my parents' bedroom and lit the candles each time he prayed, so he saw them every day. A few days went by, and my brothers were playing in my parents' bedroom. Thomas broke one of the candlesticks while they were playing. Michael and Thomas put it back together with glue, and as kids, we thought they did an excellent job.

About a month later, my father saw that someone had tampered with one of the candlesticks. As he looked further, he realized that it had been glued together; of course, he was furious. My mother let it slip that my brothers had been playing in their bedroom, and Tommy had accidentally knocked it over. Now, at the time, my mother worked the first shift and my father worked the second shift, so when we went to school, he was sleeping, and when we came home, he was working. A couple of weeks went by, and my father was still stewing about that candlestick. Unbeknownst to my mother, he went to Tommy's school and told his teacher that Tommy had a doctor's appointment, so the teacher let him take my brother out. He did not really have a doctor's appointment. My father took him home so he could beat him for breaking the candlestick. When the rest of us got home, we found Tommy under the bed, all black and blue, having soiled his pants.

1973

My father was always a good provider. Each year, he would slaughter a cow and a pig, and we would have our meat for the year. After slaughtering a cow, my parents and grandmother were wrapping the individual pieces, and they were putting them in the freezer. My father was tired or frustrated because after my mother asked him a question, he took a piece of meat that was on a bone and he hit my mother in the forehead with it, splitting her forehead wide open. I started yelling at my father and crying at the sight of my mother bleeding. My father usually had a good aim, and he threw a bone at me, but he missed. I could not figure out why he was so mean at times. The more frustrated he got, the more he took it out on his family. Most men would love to be in his situation, having a loving wife and children who looked up to him.

That summer, my godfather lived on Cape Cod. He was better off financially than most and always had a big heart. My father always sent a care package to São Miguel, Azores, for his family (never to my mother's family). My godfather called my father and said, "Why don't you guys come up, because I have some clothes that I think your family could use." It was sixty-three miles between my father's house and my godfather's house. My father called his cousin and explained the situation, and his cousin agreed to come to drive us. We had a wonderful visit with my godfather. My godfather gave the clothes to my father, along with some money to send to São Miguel, Azores. We said our goodbyes, and the nightmare began. My father and his cousin began bickering over who would get what. He immediately told his cousin to pull over and stop the car. My father began hitting his cousin, and we children were all crying. My father's cousin drove off, leaving our whole family on the sidewalk. Picture this: six people walking along the sidewalk with no idea about where we were going. My mother was trying to comfort the four boys when all of a sudden, my father punched her in the back, and she fell down. Victor tried to comfort her. Thank God my father's cousin came back a half-hour later and took us back home.

1974

My Father was exceedingly difficult to live with, especially when he drank. He loved his wine. One day, we were having dinner, and he reached over to my mother and slapped her so hard. Of course, she started to cry. She looked at him and said, "What was that for?" He never answered her. He was a mean man who abused his family to no end. Everything had to be done his way, and if it were not, he would take it out on his family. My mother never had a say because my father was the head of the household, and all decisions were made by him and only him. My brother Victor used to say only God and the six members of our family know what actually goes on behind the four walls of our home.

1975

We had a curfew every night. During the week, we had to be home at 9:00, and on the weekend it was 11:00. One night I wanted to test the water, and I got home at 1:00 in the morning. My father never gave us the keys to the house. The door was locked, so I slept in the garage in my father's 1972 Dodge Polara, in the middle of winter. At 3:00 a.m., my mother went into the garage, snuck me into the house, and gave me three shots of whiskey because I was freezing. My mother said, "Pray to God that your father is drunk and has passed out." That lady went through a lot being the wife of such a man.

1976

My grandmother was visiting from São Miguel, Azores, and was staying with us for six months. My mother was making dinner one night. My father started complaining about supper, even though we boys thought supper was good. My mother talked back to him, and he did not like it. She made a joke by saying that when a person drinks too much, their taste buds are gone. He took offense to that and slapped her, and my mother said, "May you receive the same slap from God someday." He did not like that either, so he punched her. My grandmother tried to calm him down, but he was relentless. My mother hid in the closet. He looked for her, and when he found her, he grabbed her by the hair and dragged her from room to room. My grandmother tried to stop him, but he knocked her down. I grabbed his hands so he would let her go. He stopped, took off his belt, and started to whip me. One of my neighbors called the police officers; they came, and I told them what had happened. I showed them the ball of hair that he pulled from my mother's head and the belt marks on my body. He got arrested and spent that night in jail.

1977

One Saturday night, my brother and I were out with friends, having a wonderful time, and we passed curfew. Michael looked at me and said, "We better go home before we get in trouble." I said, "We are having such a great time that I'm willing to take my chances." I was pretty popular that evening, and I did not want the fun to end. Finally, my brother said, "Joe, we better go," and I agreed. As soon as Michael turned the key to open the door, my father was waiting for us with the belt in his hand. My father lashed at me first, but Michael got the brunt of it because my parents always consider Michael to be the oldest.

1978

My father was always an ambitious person. All he wanted was to make a dollar, and he did. I really believe that if he had ever mastered the English language, he would have been a self-made millionaire. He had a fabric business at the house, and on Saturdays, he and Thomas would go door to door selling fabrics, bed sheets, comforters, and curtains. He made lots of money on the fabric while he continued working his regular job, so we would have health benefits. By this time, my father switched shifts from second to first. One evening—I will never forget this as long as I live—my father had too much to drink. He and Thomas were arguing, and he backhanded Thomas. Thomas took my mother, and they went to the fabric room and shut the plywood door. My brother Victor, who was very fit, had a weight set. My father was so outraged that he took the bar from the weight set and put it through the plywood door. It caught Thomas on the head, and there was blood everywhere. My father had health insurance that covered us, but since Thomas was under eighteen years old, he needed parental permission for treatment at the hospital. My dad did not want the medical team to know he had injured Thomas. Michael was over eighteen and was working at that time and had his own insurance, so Michael drove Thomas to the ER, and they signed Thomas in as Michael. Michael told me later that the cut was so bad that he could see Thomas's skull.

Later that year, I was around eighteen years old. It was hot, and I was home with my parents alone because my brothers were working. My father was always angry for some reason. He started to argue and began talking badly to my mother, and I stuck up for her. He began to slap me, but I curled up into a ball. He took off his belt and started to whip me, then he put the belt around my neck, and he dragged me from room to room. I could not catch my breath. Thank God the belt broke in his hand because if it had not, I believe I would have died. It left a huge imprint on my neck that was there for days. I did not want anyone to see it, so I put on a turtleneck sweater. I walked by my neighbor and said hello, and he said, "Why are you wearing a sweater on a hot day?" I said, "No reason." But he looked at my neck and saw the belt imprint, and said, "Did your father do that to you?" and I said, "Yes," and immediately I started to cry with anger.

I came home from school one afternoon, and my father asked me to do something. I looked at him and said, "Okay, I will do it later." One thing you do not say to my father is no, but I had to study, and I was tired. He started whipping and kicking me. I looked at him, bleeding, and asked him, "Do you know why I was born disabled?" He said, "No." I told him, "Michael, Thomas, and Victor are all built, and they can take you out at any time, but out of respect or fear, they do not. Me, on the other hand, if I were capable like my brothers and saw you hit my mother, I would have killed you by now. The first time that I saw you hit my mother, I would have taken you down and I would have gone to jail, but it would have been worth it." He heard me and continued the beating.

18

I got on the plane and sat near a window. I saw my brother leaving the airport, wiping his eyes. The plane took off, and I started to pray and asked the Father, our Lord, to please guide me with His Loving Hands. I arrived at LAX, Cathy and Paul picked me up, and I was in California!

The next day, they showed me around the area where they lived in Glendora, CA. It was a wonderful community. It reminded me of Bristol, RI. A couple of weeks went by, and I figured that if I could find a job, maybe just maybe I could stay a little longer. So, I went to the Department of Rehabilitation looking for work. I found a job with A.Q.M., which stands for Advocates for the Quiet Minority. I found a job as a counselor. I was very proud of that because it dealt with mostly handicapped clients, and I guess I was an expert when it came to being disabled.

I had a job, a job that I enjoyed, and they enjoyed me. Cathy and Paul told me, "Joe, you have been living with us for about four months. What are your plans?" I told them that I wanted to stay in California, and could they please help me find an apartment. Paul had a friend by the name of Terry Staley, who owned his own home. At first, Terry was skeptical about taking me in as a roommate because of my disability. I told him to give me a chance, and if things didn't work out, I would move back to Rhode Island. After thinking about it for a week, he agreed.

He told me what he expected, and I accepted. When he told me that on Saturday everyone does chores, I looked at him puzzled and asked him, "What chores?" He explained that on Saturdays, Steve (our other roommate) and Terry cleaned the house. I grabbed him aside and told him my mother did all my chores. I didn't know where to begin. He took me aside and said, "OK, I will teach you."

Saturday, I usually liked to sleep in, but that was not the way Terry did things. He believed that the earlier we started, the earlier we could get done. My first chore was to do the bathroom. I agreed, and I was done in fifteen minutes, and he showed me how to do it right, and it took me three hours. I was tired! He also said that Saturday was laundry day, and he tried to show me how to do it. But I told him that I watched my mother over the years, and I knew exactly what to do. I should have listened to him because I ruined my clothes. The same thing happened when I tried to iron my clothes. Finally, I started to get smart and listened to Steve and Terry. It was like having to grow up all over again, because when I lived in Rhode Island, I was spoiled rotten. My parents did everything for me. I really didn't know what to do or how to do it. With time, I adjusted, and I did well, but it was a tough adjustment.

I was in touch with my family often, and I missed them very much. I wanted to visit my family for Christmas and New Year's. I got permission from work, and I came home for the holidays. It seemed different because, naturally, I had developed my personal life. I even became a pretty good cook. My parents were pleasantly surprised that I developed these skills. I stayed about ten days. At the same time, the United Cerebral Palsy had their telethon, and they wanted to do a feature about me, so I stayed another ten days with permission from work. It was nice to be back because these were my roots; this was where it all began. Deep down inside, I wanted to stay and not go back to California, but for some reason, a voice was telling me I had to go back. After about twenty days in Rhode Island, it was time to go back to California.

I had been thinking of finding a new place to live, but I knew I would need a roommate to help with expenses. I got back to work, and one of the counselors at AQM told me that one of his clients was looking for a roommate. The client, a twenty-three-year-old man named Rick, was schizophrenic and already had an apartment. He just needed someone to keep an eye on him. They asked me if I was interested. The way I looked at it was that a lot of people had been good to me, and it was time to give back. Besides, I could be a positive role model, so I agreed. I explained the situation to Terry, and he agreed it was a win-win situation. I met my new roommate, Rick, along with his parents, and we hit it off well.

I was going to a church by the name of Calvary Chapel. Two of the church members, whom I came to love very much, were named Robert Messerschmidt and William Simonian. They were more like the uncles that I never had. Whenever I was down, one of them was always around to pick me up. Those two gentlemen really exemplified unconditional love. Bob and Bill thought I should move in with Rick and be a positive role model, and maybe I could become a good influence in his life. We all agreed that this could be a wonderful experience for both of us. Besides, I really didn't have anything to lose and everything to gain.

Rick's parents were very helpful with everything that Rick and I needed. They had furnished the apartment completely, so that all I had to do was move in. Rick and I sat down and talked about what we expected from each other. He was a wonderful young man and really didn't want much. All he wanted was someone to look up to. I did all the cooking, and he cleaned, and every Saturday, we would divide the chores that needed to be done. I was scared at first because he looked up to me, and I really didn't want to disappoint him.

I went to bed one evening, and I couldn't sleep. I was tossing and turning, and sleep would not come. I started to think about the Olympic competition that was held in Los Angeles in 1984. I started to cry because I love sports, and if only I had my physical abilities, maybe I would be good enough to compete with the world. The more I thought about it, the angrier I got. I believe the United States won 132 medals that year for the summer games. I looked up to Heaven and shouted, "God, it might have been 133 medals, but we are not going to find out!" and cried myself to sleep.

Then, as if in a dream, I saw myself with all my physical attributes intact. It was like my head on someone else's body. Although it was like a dream, I felt fully awake with all my senses functioning normally. I was in the triathlon at the Olympics, which was composed of three events: running, jumping, and weightlifting. I saw myself winning all three events and winning the gold medal. I was running around the track with the flag of the United States of America draped around my body, and everyone there was chanting "USA, USA, USA, etc." I went to the platform to receive my gold medal, and suddenly everyone in the Los Angeles Coliseum disappeared at the twinkling of an eye. The place turned dark, and I was confused and screamed, "Where's my glory? I just won the gold medal; people should be praising me!" Suddenly, I didn't see anything, but I heard a voice that said, "My dear child, these people are going to remember you just for a while, but I will never forget you." I woke up and I got on my knees and thanked God. That was the night that I came to grips with my disability and finally won the war that had been raging within me.

19

I kept in touch with my family constantly, and I told them about Rick. They were very happy, but at the same time, they were very skeptical. They wanted me home, especially my mother. I couldn't leave because I really believed that I had a job to do. People gave me so much over the years, and it was time that I gave something back to society.

One day, I went shopping at the mall for clothes and spent a few hours there. I always loved to shop. Most men hate to shop, but I love it. I took the bus home, and it was full of people, so this young lady got up and gave me her seat. I was very impressed because not often does a lady get up and offer her seat to a man. I kept looking at her and she at me. I said to myself, no matter where she gets off, I will follow and talk to her, and maybe ask for her telephone number. This had to be my lucky night because she got off at my stop. I talked to her and invited her for a drink, and she declined. I was also curious as to why she gave up her seat. She responded by saying that I was disabled, and she didn't want me to fall. Talking to her, I didn't think I was disabled. From that moment on, I thought that she was very special. I asked her where she lived and if I could have her telephone number. She gave me her telephone number, but she didn't tell me her address. She did tell me where she worked, and she said if I wanted to take her out, then I would have to meet her after work.

I couldn't sleep that night thinking about her, I tossed and turned, but no sleep. I finally got up and called her and asked her what her name was. She told me it was Josephine Scott. I also asked her why she didn't tell me her name before, and she said, "Because you didn't ask," and I guess I hadn't. We talked for about half an hour. Finally, we said good night, and I went to sleep. I thought she was very special, and I was so happy to talk with her, and I didn't feel disabled.

The following week, I called her home and asked her if she wanted to go out that night. She said yes, but I had to pick her up at work. I tried again to get her home address, but she wouldn't give it to me. I picked her up after work, and she looked surprised because she didn't think that I was going to show up. We went to the movies and then got a bite to eat after the show. It was really a wonderful night; we hit it off well. I finally got to know her home address when I walked her home. I asked her why she wouldn't give me her home address before. She told me guys like me would just take advantage of women like her, and she had to know for sure that I was a nice guy.

I guess she liked me, because she seemed assured that I was not going to take advantage of her. I knew right away that I liked her and told her things that I wouldn't tell my best friend. She was a wonderful lady, and I was totally falling head over heels for her. I kissed her good night, and I kissed her again and again. I never felt this way; I was completely in her control, but I couldn't tell her because I didn't want her to know. All that I knew was that she was a wonderful lady and I liked her very much. The more we talked, the more I wanted her, and I never felt like this before; I was completely like pudding.

The next morning, she called to thank me for a wonderful evening. Inside, I was chuckling because I thought I should be thanking her for the best night I'd had since I had been in California. We went out a couple of days later because I wanted to make sure that wonderful feeling that I had was the same feeling that I had before.

I told her about Rick and explained to her the situation that I was in. She thought what I was doing was great. She met Rick and they hit it off very well. In fact, when I was working on her day off, she spent the day with Rick. That really didn't surprise me because that was her way: always helping someone who was less fortunate than she was.

A few weeks went by, and I received a telephone call from CLIMB (Center for Living Independence for the Multi-handicapped Blind), offering me a new job. Even though I had a good job, I felt that I could do better at this new position, but there was a catch: they wanted me to work the second shift, from 3 p.m. to 11 p.m. I told them I would get back to them in a couple of days. I wanted the job, but I also had a commitment to Rick, and working second shift meant leaving Rick alone at night. Who was going to watch him in the evenings? I discussed my situation with Josephine, and she asked me if I was going to take the job. I told her that I wanted to, but I thought I should reject the offer because Rick came first. She said, "Take the job, and when I get out of work, I will go to your apartment and stay with Rick until you come home." I looked at her and said, "What did I do to deserve you?" She smiled and said, "Joseph, now that I am here, you don't have to do everything. I would like to share your load." I knew then that she was the woman with whom I wanted to spend the rest of my life.

Now that we had a plan, we needed to tell Rick, because if he said no, then I couldn't accept the job. When Josephine visited the apartment to see me, she would arrive after Rick had gone to bed. This was our private time. Often, however, if Rick heard her, he would get up, because he liked to visit with her. I think Rick looked up to Josephine, and he liked her in his own innocent way.

Josephine and I came in, and Rick was watching television. When he saw her, he quickly turned off the TV and sat near her. I told him that we needed to talk, and he got afraid, because he thought I was going to get mad at him because of the way he acted when he was around Josephine. We told him what we had discussed earlier, and he breathed a sigh of relief. We told him that whatever Josephine asked him to do, he was expected to do, just as if it were me.

My new job at CLIMB was the position of residential counselor. It was very challenging because all the students were blind. These blind students were simply amazing because even though they couldn't see, they were very in tune with everything around them. Working with them showed me, once again, that everyone has the right to live their lives to the fullest, no matter what disadvantages they may have. The students were dependent on me, and it was important that I acted in a manner that earned their respect. Again, I was given the message that even though I had disabilities, there were others with different struggles.

I like to think I had a positive influence on these students. There was one whom I really enjoyed being around. His name was Gary, and he was special to me because of his positive attitude. He never said "no." He always said "yes" or "I'll try." He thought my skin was orange. I asked him why, and he said that an orange always smelled good, and that I always smelled good, so I must have orange skin.

I really loved that job because I knew I made a difference in the lives of the students I worked with, and I counted my blessings. I was also giving thanks to God up above, because for the first time, I was grateful for my cerebral palsy. I realized that by accepting that I had this condition, it was helping me to be a better person. I told Josephine that I felt like I was finally on the right track, but she disagreed. She told me that I'd always been on the right track; I just hadn't stopped to smell the roses. Maybe she was right. All I knew was that I was having fun and enjoying life, and things were clicking for me. Besides, now I had someone that I really trusted with my life completely, and I knew she was always there; she was my best friend. Everything was going well, and I didn't think it could have been any better.

20

I called my family back in Rhode Island and explained the situation because they were really expecting me to move back to Rhode Island. When I told them about Josephine and about my new job, they were very happy, but by the same token, they didn't like the timing. They were expecting me back, but I was in love with Josephine and not ready to leave, plus I felt a responsibility towards Rick.

Rick was having a great time because Josephine was doing everything for him, and basically, he was getting lazy. When I found out, I went through the roof and got angry with Rick, but I was more upset with Josephine because I thought she knew better. She told me that I had to ease up, and she was right. Because I was disabled, I felt I had to do everything correctly, and I was measuring Rick's performance against my own. She pointed that out to me, and she was right. It is amazing what a person whom you trust can teach you if you listen to them. I would never have thought that I was being so tough on Rick until Josephine pointed it out. The more I listened to her, the more I learned. She always taught by example, and not by preaching.

By now, I was completely in love with her. By the same token, I wanted to go back to Rhode Island. She always knew without a doubt when something was wrong. She could see that I was in conflict, and she asked me about it. I tried to deny it, but she knew better. I told her I was falling in love with her, but someday I wanted to go back to Rhode Island and live back East. She told me, "Joseph, I am totally in love with you, and no matter where you go, I will follow." She was a wonderful person with a big heart. She was always there for someone who needed her. I often wonder where she got the energy and the strength. Besides being a manager in a maternity shop, she always had time for others, without reservations. I was blessed to have this beautiful lady in my life.

Rick's parents became concerned about Josephine because Rick would go to his parents' home for the weekend, and apparently, he would talk about Josephine. Maybe it was my fault, but I had not told his parents about Josephine. I had figured they were going to meet her eventually. When they did, they liked her, but they were still uneasy. That bothered me because I didn't think Rick could find a better person to hang around with, and she was a wonderful woman without the physical limitations that I had.

My parents wanted to know if I was going to come home for the holidays. I told them that I was, and that I was going to bring my girlfriend. They hesitated but finally agreed. I had been wanting to go back East, and I really wanted to show Josephine what the East was like. Even though I had everything I needed in California, I still missed what the East Coast had to offer.

One night, I took Josephine and Rick out to dinner, and took something out of my pocket and gave it to her. It was a diamond ring. I asked her to marry me, and she accepted. Now Rick was happy and sad at the same time, and we asked him what was wrong. He said that he was very happy for both of us, but now he felt like a third wheel. Josephine and I had talked about Rick's future, and we had agreed that he would always need someone to watch over him.

By now, we had grown to love Rick as our little brother. We told him that when the time came for us to move back to the East Coast, he was more than welcome to come and live with us. He smiled and said he would like to do that.

When Rick tried to explain to his parents what Josephine and I discussed at dinner, they got the impression that we wanted to take Rick away from them, and that was the farthest thing from the truth. Since Josephine had been in our lives, I had tried to introduce her to Rick's parents quite a few times. They always had some excuse as to why they couldn't meet her. Now his parents wanted to meet with Josephine and me, and I refused. My pride was telling me that if she wasn't good enough to meet before, then why now? Rick's parents decided to take Rick home and gave me the choice of keeping the apartment or closing it up. I realized I needed to make one last effort and tried to have them meet with us, but they refused. I told them I would be moving out and asked for two weeks to find another place, to which they agreed.

I couldn't find an apartment, so when Josephine asked me to move in with her, I agreed. If we were going to get married, why make two monthly rent payments? Besides, it would be a good thing because even though I could take care of myself, I would always need someone around to help me with the things I couldn't do. By this time, we were really in love, both of us were working, and nothing could be better. The one thing that I didn't like was that we worked different shifts. It really bothered me because I only saw her on the weekends. Usually, Sunday was church day, and the day to visit friends and family. So that left Saturdays as the one day of the week we had time together.

We were close to going back East for our visit, and Josephine was getting nervous because she had never flown before. I tried to comfort her, and she looked into my eyes and said, "Joseph, when I look into your eyes, I feel this real sense of security." I knew I had something with her because that was how I felt when I looked into her eyes. Her family did not like the idea of me taking their daughter away from them, especially during the holidays. I came to find out later that Josephine and her family were very close-knit. I tried to be understanding, but by the same token, we were only going for two weeks. Besides, I thought it was time for Josephine to get to know my family, too.

Thomas picked us up at Logan Airport in Boston, and when he saw Josephine, he made her feel right at home. We arrived at my parents' house, and my family was happy to see me and their future daughter-in-law. My parents made every effort to make her feel at home and accommodate all of her needs. If they didn't have something, they would get it. At this time of year, it was snowing. Josephine had never seen snow, and she loved it.

She called her family back in California and told them she was having a wonderful time. That didn't sit too well with her family. She didn't tell me, but I could see it in her eyes. Even though I tried to get her to tell me, she insisted everything was fine. The next few days, my brothers took us around and showed her Bristol, and she loved it. Again, I told her that we would get married in California, and after our honeymoon, we would go straight to Rhode Island, and again, she agreed. Deep down in my heart, however, I felt that she had not told her family about our plans, but I knew in time she would.

21

Christmas came along, and everyone began to open gifts. To Josephine's surprise, and quite honestly to mine, everybody in my family bought her a gift. After seeing my happiness, they had instantly accepted Josephine as a family member, which surprised me and warmed my heart. My parents loved her because they saw the caring that was within her. At dinner, Josephine never sat down without making my plate first. My mother was especially impressed when Josephine clipped my fingernails, one of the things I couldn't do for myself. My mother approached me and said, "Joe, you have found someone who really loves you." I looked at my mom and said, "Mom, I am blessed, and the best thing is that I know it!"

Manny Pimental, my friend from the United Cerebral Palsy, came to meet Josephine and instantly fell in love with her. I came to find out a couple of months later that Manny took Josephine aside and explained what cerebral palsy was. He told her I would live with this condition the rest of my life. She told him, "Manny, I'm glad that he has cerebral palsy, because without it, I don't think he'd be half the man that he is today." Manny returned with tears in his eyes. I tried to find out what they had said to each other, but he just looked at me and said, "Joe, you couldn't find a better woman to spend your life with."

I guess he was still looking out for me and didn't want me to get hurt, because he loved me like a son.

At night, Josephine and I talked about the future and how much she loved the East Coast, especially Bristol. If I had my way, she would have stayed here, and I would have gone back to California to gather our belongings and come back for good. But she didn't think that would sit well with her family, and she was probably right; her family would probably have hated me if we had done that to them.

On New Year's Eve, my brother Michael and his wife Maria took us out to dinner. We discussed many things over dinner, including finding an apartment when we returned. At the time, Michael and Maria owned three apartments, and he told us not to worry about an apartment because he would let one of his tenants go, and we could move in. We liked that because Josephine and Maria got along very well, plus, who better to help you settle in than family? Josephine and Maria had spent a lot of time together, and I was glad that Josephine would have a friend already when we moved back to Bristol.

Josephine called her family to wish them Happy New Year, but again, she seemed to change when she got off the phone. I tried to be understanding, but she would not open up to me. I didn't put any pressure on her because I figured she would tell me when she was ready. All I could do was be there for her whenever she needed me, but deep down in my heart, I knew something was wrong.

We finally talked, and she admitted that her family didn't want her to move to the East Coast. I became angry because she was caught in the middle, but she had to make up her mind between her family and her future husband. She was a very caring person who would much rather hurt herself than the other person. I never knew a person could be so caring, but I witnessed it with my own eyes. She had a hard time making decisions when her loved ones were involved and would ponder and ponder. She was an unusual woman, and I was very blessed to have her. I had never met a person like that. She taught me about a world I never knew existed, and I kept falling more in love with her every day. She taught me the concept of self-giving.

During the remaining days before we returned to California, we simply tried to enjoy each other's company. Deep down, I knew that when we got back, it would be a tough battle, but I was confident in my abilities, and I was willing to do anything to protect the woman I loved. No matter what happened, I was determined to overcome the obstacles that stood in our path to a happy life. We said our goodbyes to the family, and Michael pulled me aside and told me to be patient and just let everything fall into place. I just looked at him and told him to get that apartment ready because I was coming back married, and that I wasn't going to let anyone stand in the way of my true happiness. All my life, I had been fighting for what I wanted, and this was no exception.

Thomas took us to the airport and told Josephine, "Welcome to the family!" and thanked her for bringing happiness into my life. We got into the plane, and when we took off, I looked at her and squeezed her hand, because I knew we were headed for uncharted waters. I still felt confident that we would be able to handle the situation.

A couple of friends picked us up at the airport when we arrived in California. We got home, and Josephine took a nap. I, of course, was wired so I couldn't go to sleep. My mind was in Rhode Island and our future. I couldn't wait to start a new life with her in Rhode Island, and in time, I knew we would have children. Josephine would be a great mother because she has a wonderful way with kids.

Monday morning rolled around, and she got up and went

to take a shower, so I tried to make breakfast. It wasn't as good as she usually made it. It didn't taste that great, and she said, "I still have a little money, why don't I take you out and buy you breakfast?" I asked her if my breakfast was really that bad, and she said, "Joseph, my darling, the breakfast isn't bad, but I just want to go out and enjoy the beautiful weather." At the restaurant, she told me not to make breakfast anymore because it was something she really enjoyed doing every morning.

I went to work that afternoon, and it was great to see everyone, especially the students. I really missed them because, for some reason, I drew strength from them. It took me a while to get into the swing of things, having been gone for two weeks. It was a tough night, but I managed to survive. The person who replaced me on the next shift was going to be late that night, so I called home and told Josephine I'd be late. When I got in at 1:30 that morning, I thought she'd be in bed, but when I opened the door, she was waiting for me. I was really surprised because she had to work the next morning. I asked her why she was still up, and she said that she needed to cook my dinner. I told her I could do that, and she said, "Remember breakfast this morning?" After I had eaten, I went to the living room and sat down on the couch. She sat down beside me and said she couldn't sleep. I put my arms around her and told her I must be one of the most blessed men that ever walked on the earth. She started crying and said, "Joseph, thank you for making my dreams come true." Then I started to cry. I kept talking, and I thought she was listening, but she had fallen asleep in my arms. I thought about taking her to the bedroom, but she looked so peaceful that I didn't move an inch.

The next morning, my arm was sore because she had slept on it, but I enjoyed that pain because all I could see was her peacefully sleeping in my arms. She made me a wonderful, tasty breakfast, and then I accompanied her on the bus to work. After dropping her off, I went to the florist and ordered a dozen roses and had them shipped to her workplace. When she received them, she called me to thank me. However, I thought I should be the one to thank her because she was such a wonderful person, and the roses I bought her would never match her beauty. I even remember what I wrote on the card. It went something like this: "To the woman I never thought existed until I laid my eyes on you."

When I met her, I had a beard, and one day she asked me to shave it off. I wanted to, but the only reason I grew one in the first place was because every time I shaved, I used to cut my face all up. I told her why I had the beard, and she took my hand, sat me in the chair, went to the bathroom, and got the shaving cream and razor. She asked me if I wanted to shave off my beard, and I told her I did. She said that from that day forward, she would shave me every day.

I was stunned because she was willing to take time away from her busy schedule to cater to me. I tried to tell her that it wasn't necessary, but the more I tried to convince her that I could do it on my own, the more she insisted on doing it. I finally gave in and agreed to let her do it. Now, every day, I was clean-shaven without any nicks or cuts, and I even looked younger than she did. Whatever she did for me, she never complained and did it with a smile on her face. I often wondered why she did all these things without complaining, and she told me that whatever she did for me couldn't ever make up for what I had done for her. That really didn't make sense because I really didn't do that much for her, so she had to be mistaken, but she insisted that I was the one mistaken. What more did I want? I have everything that a man could ever want in a woman, plus I felt like I had my life in order, and that my disability had turned out to be a blessing.

22

I came home from work one Friday, and she was preparing my dinner, and I saw a picnic basket in the kitchen. I asked her what it was for, and she said it was for the picnic that the two of us were supposedly going on. I played dumb right away and told her that she had the weeks mixed up, that it was the next week. She said, "Joseph, can't you even lie straight? What is the reason you can't go tomorrow?" I put my arm around her and took her into the living room and told her that I had invited one of my students to spend the weekend with us. She smiled at me and said, "That's OK, he can come with us on the picnic!" She was always flexible in any situation, and I thought she was remarkable when it came to things like that.

The student who stayed with us was Gary Rydingsword, and he couldn't stop thanking us for this time together. Josephine and I looked at each other and shrugged our shoulders, and asked him why he was thanking us every ten minutes. He said that when Josephine and I had gone to Rhode Island for the holidays, none of his family had even come to visit him. That really bothered us because Gary and I were very close, and I really liked him very much. When you work with people who are less fortunate than you, you try to divide your time evenly among everyone. However, there is always someone who inspires you to go the extra mile, and Gary was that special person for me. He was a man, but still had that child mentality, and that was what made him special. He didn't ask for much, but he did make one request, and that was when we moved back to Rhode Island to take him for the holidays. Josephine and I looked at each other and told him we would do that, but we would have to get permission from the school. We went to the administration office and explained what Gary wanted to do and said that all responsibility would be ours. They said that whatever Gary wanted to do was up to him. They also told me that he was well off, so he had money to cover his expenses. That didn't really matter to me if he was happy. We loved spending time with him because he was a joy to be with.

Josephine and I were trying to get on with our plans for the wedding, and Josephine's mother (Sharon) tried to get involved. I really didn't mind, but what upset me was the way she demanded everything. I finally looked at her and asked her who was getting married, her or her daughter? I guess she didn't like that too much, but I really didn't care. What I wanted was just to marry her daughter; everything else didn't matter. I was under pressure to do what other people wanted, and I was sick of it. I just wanted the two of us to have a nice wedding and to live a quiet, simple life. Even my parents had certain things in mind for the wedding. I told them that we would consider it, and I thanked them, but I just wanted this to be simple and not to go so far in the hole financially that it would take years to get out of it. I told her mother that she and my family were not going to ruin our wedding. I would appreciate their input, but Josephine and I would make the ultimate decisions, whether people liked it or not. I really believe that day was the beginning of the end of her mother ever liking me again. I tried to explain to her that I was going to be married only once, and I wanted it to be the best for her daughter and me, and whatever decisions Josephine and I made would be final. I guess she didn't take too kindly to that remark, and I was sorry I even said it.

We were discussing a wedding date, and I said, "Why don't we get married on your birthday?" Josephine's birthday just happened to be on a Sunday. Her birthday was on June 20, and she thought it was very romantic and thoughtful. However, deep down in my heart, I had a totally different reason. My thinking was that if we got married on her birthday, I wouldn't forget the two occasions, and plus, instead of buying two gifts, I would only buy one. Plus, when one occasion comes, I would also remember the other occasion. We men forget these special days over the years, but unfortunately, women never forget. She gave me a hug and said, "Joseph, don't think that one gift will cover both occasions. It's going to cost you dearly!" I knew that every year was going to be expensive after she said that.

Josephine's sister, Mary, used to manage the apartments where we lived, and she had a master key to all the apartments. Josephine and she were very close, and whatever they had, they used to share. One day, I opened the door to my apartment, and I found her sister going through the pantry. I looked at her and said, "What are you doing here?" She said, "I needed some sugar, so I came and got some." I told her that unless Josephine or I were home, she didn't have any business in our apartment. When Josephine got home, I wanted her to explain to me why everyone shared everything with each other. She said that she was the only one working constantly, and basically, she was the only source of income for her family. That night we went to her mother's house, and her mother asked me what had happened with Mary. I tried to explain to her mother that if we are not home, then you have two choices: either wait for us or come back later when we are home. Josephine's mother told me that each of her children had a key to each other's apartments. I totally disagreed with that because I didn't think it was right for everyone to be able to just come and go as they pleased. I told Josephine to leave the keys that did not belong to her. Her mother and I got into a big argument about our different upbringings.

I told her that I like my privacy, and that I didn't need anyone to have a key to my apartment. Her mother told Josephine and me to leave, and I said, "Fine, but before I leave, I would like the key to our place." She threw it down the stairs. She told Josephine not to expect her at the wedding. When we got home, Josephine was upset, and I tried to be understanding, but I was upset, too, and we started yelling at each other. Finally, I got up, grabbed my jacket, and went for a walk. An hour later, I came back. I hugged her and said I was sorry, but I really didn't appreciate the way her family treated her. That wasn't the way I was brought up. I also told her I love to give, but when people expect things, that's when I stop giving. Her family depended on Josephine, and I think they were angry at me because I was taking Josephine away from them. When they found out that we were getting married and moving back to Rhode Island, they were upset. They were even more upset that I was a stranger who was trying to steal their daughter and sister. We got along great, and I was convinced that I was doing the right thing. Josephine and I had just clicked, right from the start. It would be a shame if we didn't wind up together because no matter what we did, even if it was the wrong decision in the short run, it would ultimately be the right decision in the long run.

Unfortunately, her mother got sick, and Josephine, with everything else she had to do, was pushed into taking care of her. Now, I knew how much Josephine worked, and with this added to it, I just felt it would be too much for her. I was pretty upset because I didn't have a voice in it. But this was Josephine's mother, and Josephine wanted and accepted the challenge. Josephine came to me and told me that it would mean spending some time away from me, but she gave me the final choice. My head was saying, "No, don't do it," but my heart was saying, "Why not? You are the best person to care for someone." So, I told her, "Honey, if you think you can do it, then I am not going to stop you." I was angry at her sisters and brother because I thought that since they were very close, the responsibility should be divided equally, and it wasn't. That is what angered me the most.

I also knew that this inconvenience would put a halt to our future plans together. Day after day, I noticed Josephine getting run down trying to care for our lives and her mother. I told her we needed to talk, so try to find one of your family members to stay with your mother, so we can at least have dinner and spend a couple of hours together. We went to dinner, and naturally, she looked as wonderful as the day we met. I told her that she needed some time to herself, including from me, and, of course, she disagreed. Unfortunately, when she had her mind set, she was very stubborn. Her thinking was that whenever she started something, she would finish it. I was really enjoying the time with her, even though she didn't agree with any of my suggestions. I said, Josephine, your mother comes first now, and we come second. Instead of going back and forth from your mother's apartment to ours, why don't you just stay with your mother full-time? She said no because she didn't know who would take care of me. That was the kind of person she was, always thinking of others.

I told her that before she came along, I took very good care of myself. To be totally honest, she kind of took over my everyday routine. Every time I tried to help, I always got in the way, except on Thursday mornings, when our shifts were different and I could be alone. During the week, when I got up, I would find my breakfast in the microwave with instructions on how to heat it, and my coffee pot full of coffee, because I am still a huge coffee drinker to this day. But for some reason, on Thursdays, she made more noise than an army of men, so I had to get up. I told her to let me sleep, but the more I told her, the less she listened, and the more noise she made.

23

For some unknown reason, beyond a shadow of a doubt, men always get stuck taking out the garbage. It doesn't matter what the excuse is, we men can't think of a good reason not to do it, so we always take it out, like good boys. I always had to get up on Thursday mornings to take out the trash, and I always did it with a smile, but deep down, I was complaining to myself and wondering why I had to do it. Josephine had this knack; whenever she wanted something done, she always pushed the right buttons. To be honest, I think she could have pushed the wrong buttons, and it would have still come out right. I am convinced that women in any relationship can out-think their partners.

I am also convinced that women let their partners win in most situations, to feed their ego. We men, deep inside, are gloating, saying to ourselves, "I won, and you lost," when the woman knows exactly when to push the right button or pull the right string. A perfect example is when the two partners get into an argument. Women bring up a lot of pertinent information that relates to the subject that you are arguing about; men just shut up like a clam. We decide to take a walk to digest what our counterpart has just told us, and we come to realize that they were right all along. What do we do next? We call the florist to send our wonderful partners flowers just to say, "I'm sorry." But because of our ego, we never say "I'm sorry" for whatever the reason for the disagreement was. Instead, we apologize for something totally different. Josephine loved flowers, and whenever she wanted some, she would bring up a disagreement. After we got done, ten minutes later, I would be on the phone, and that call was usually expensive. Believe me, when we start to think that we have the upper hand in a relationship, that's when we usually get into trouble!

Josephine left to stay with her mother for a couple of months, just until her mother got back on her feet. I also convinced her that I could take care of myself, and if I needed anything, Josephine was just a phone call away. Plus, I knew that Josephine would give her mother better care than all her siblings put together. It was going to be tough for me, especially when Josephine had done everything (except take out the garbage), but I did have the ability to do whatever needed to be done.

During her lunch hour, Josephine used to come home and check up on me, to see if I needed anything, and so we could spend some time together. It was strange not having her around. Again, I had to adjust to my lifestyle with minor alterations. On the weekend, I wanted Josephine around just to spend some quality time with her, but that was difficult, especially with the way things got dumped on her without any choice. The way she was, she couldn't say no, and that really bothered me. It got to the point that I became upset with her. I really wanted to put in my two cents, but Josephine said she would handle it, so I let it ride.

One weekend, Josephine found one of her sisters to stay with her mother for a night. I had the whole night planned, with dinner and just kicking up our feet and doing nothing. Suddenly, we received a phone call from her sister saying something had happened and Josephine needed to go. I would have bought that story except that it happened way too often. I grabbed the telephone and told her sister that we are going out and you'll have to make other arrangements because we couldn't help her, and I hung up the phone. Naturally, Josephine was pretty upset with me, so I got ready because we were leaving for dinner. Josephine looked at me and started crying, and said that she was not going out, she was going to stay home. I looked at her and said, "I have waited three weeks to take you out, and now you don't want to go?" Again, she said no, and we proceeded to get into a big argument. I stormed out.

I went to a bar and started having a drink, but I felt bad getting mad at Josephine, and I tried to call her, but there was no answer. I had a second drink and tried to call again, but still no answer. I ordered another and then another, and by this point, I was feeling no pain. I got up to call her again, but this time I looked at the quarter and said, "To hell with it" and sat down.

A lady came and sat next to me, trying to start a conversation. I really wasn't in the mood to talk to anyone, never mind a stranger that I really didn't know. She said, "You are cocky that you won't even talk to me." I said, "I am not cocky. I just had a heated argument with the woman that I love, and I just want to be left alone." I took my last sip, left the bartender a tip, and told the woman good night.

I was walking and I was thinking how blessed I was to have a lady like Josephine in my life. I also asked myself why we always hurt the people that we love. It came to me that when we meet someone, we keep things simple. As a relationship grows, we tend to make things more complicated, and that's when trouble starts. No matter what the circumstances, by nature, we try to take over intellectually when it should be done through feelings and emotions. However, I think that at some point in everyone's lives, those feelings and emotions surrender to intellect, and that's when complications set in. I knew what made Josephine happy, and that meant going back to basics. I also knew how much I really loved her and that nothing else mattered. I was going to really concentrate and stay focused on her and me, because after we got married, we were going back to Rhode Island, where we could start fresh, just the two of us.

24

Josephine's mother was getting better, and our wedding plans were going well. I contacted my family, who were all excited and ready for the wedding to take place. We contacted the pastor at our church so we could go through marriage counseling. We contacted the hall where the reception was going to take place and started getting our guest list for the reception together. Since I was planning on getting married only once, I really wanted this to be special. I really didn't mind the cost; I wanted my wedding day to be very special. Unfortunately, her family wanted a simple wedding with very few guests. I totally objected because even though I came from the East Coast, I had a lot of friends who wanted to come out to the wedding. We had some money saved, and I was willing to spend it.

With everything going on with her family, Josephine was having second thoughts about moving to Rhode Island. Her family was pretty upset about us getting married and going back there, and on one level, I guess I can't blame them. But by the same token, I felt I had every right to choose where to live with my wife, plus we had talked about going back to Rhode Island numerous times, so I thought we had settled it, and really didn't see the point of further discussion. To this day, I believe that day by day, Josephine's family persuaded her heart not to go to Rhode Island. I knew that once I was married, her family would not be able to stand in our way. Josephine was totally confused between her family and me, and was in the middle of all this chaos. All I wanted was to start a new life with Josephine and someday have children. As far as I was concerned, our wedding day was so far away that it seemed like an eternity. For some reason, her family disliked me. Could it be the fact that I was taking their precious family member away from them? Whatever the reason, I just wanted to start fresh away from all this. I knew deep down it was really bothering Josephine because she was being torn between her family and the man that she loved. Ultimately, she had a decision to make.

One night after work, I came home, and she was waiting for me. She smiled and gave me a kiss. For some inexplicable reason, she looked different than other nights. After I ate my dinner, we went to the living room to spend some time together. She told me that when we were blessed with children, she would like to adopt a handicapped child. I was speechless because I knew the responsibilities my own mother went through, and now she wanted that same responsibility. I asked her why. She responded by saying that if we didn't adopt a child, then we would be doing that handicapped child a disservice. I was completely shocked because here is a young woman speaking like a wise older woman. It also showed me how unrelenting this woman's unselfishness was, and she was all mine! She was a completely remarkable woman whom I was totally in love with. Finally, I gave her the decision to make. I said if she decided to adopt a handicapped child, I would support her. I also told her that she already knew my feelings toward handicapped children, and that the decision would have to be hers and hers alone. I told her that I wanted us to have a biological child first, simply because I wanted to see an offspring of mine. An extension of me that did not have physical limitations. She told me that whenever I talked about my own child, my face lit up like a Christmas tree. I told her that was because deep down in my heart, my goal was to have a child or children, knowing that they were going to be physically normal.

When Josephine and I were alone, everything was perfect, but with her family around, it was totally the opposite. It really bothered me a lot because I didn't have full control of the situation. It just irked me that whenever her family needed something, Josephine was always there for them. I was always taught that if you wanted something, you would work for it. To this day, I still feel that is good common sense. Whenever they needed something, she would jump right away to help them. That was her nature, always trying to help someone who was in need. The danger always starts when people try to take advantage of a situation. I really believe that her family took advantage of her, and that bothered me to no end.

We resumed making plans for the wedding, and I noticed Josephine was hesitating because she knew that after we got married, it was off to the East Coast. She wanted to move the wedding date, but I declined, because everything in Rhode Island was in motion, plus I couldn't wait to go back. Josephine wanted to move the wedding date because I think her family was pressuring her. I think she thought that by moving the wedding date, her family and I could settle our differences, but unfortunately, that never happened.

One day after work, I came in and saw Josephine crying, so I went to her to see what the matter was. She asked me how much I really loved her. I told her if a car was coming towards her, I would push her out of the way and let it hit me instead. She told me, "Let's get married and live in California." I said no and told her that we had always discussed, after getting married, settling back in Rhode Island. It was something we had talked about throughout our relationship. It wasn't like it was anything new; she already knew that I wanted to go back and that I wanted her to come with me. Deep down, I knew I had lost her to her family; I couldn't compete with that. Josephine had a choice to make: either her family or her future husband.

I gave my two weeks' notice at work. I felt that it was time to come back to Rhode Island. I also believed that Josephine was going to go back with me. Those next two weeks were going to be hell in my life. I went to the travel agency and booked my flight; if Josephine was going to come with me, then all I had to do was call the agency for another ticket. During those two weeks, I tried everything in my power to convince her to come with me, but the ultimate decision would be hers. I started thanking everybody that I met in California. I knew it was going to be hard to leave, especially if Josephine didn't come with me. I began to pack my belongings into boxes to be shipped out by UPS.

I told the students that I was leaving. Naturally, we were all sad, but the students thanked me for coming into their lives. I was going to miss everybody, but especially Gary. He was the one student I was going to miss the most. I really enjoyed the time we shared together, and I could see how much he had grown. I started to cry because I knew I wasn't coming back. I told him good-bye, and he said he would see me the next day. Unfortunately, he didn't have any concept of what was going on.

I had another week to convince Josephine to come with me. I told her that she would visit California once a year. I might or might not accompany her, but she would go every year and visit her family. She always knew that whatever I told her, I would always keep my word, plus, I really thought she would have had a wonderful life in Rhode Island. All my belongings were ready to be shipped. Knowing that I was leaving in a few days, I had to make my best pitch. The last couple of nights we spent together, I tried to convince her that we were made for each other. She said, "You are right, but my family needs me." I responded by saying, "What about what I need?" She told me that I would change my mind at the last minute. I looked at her and started to cry, and so did she. We loved each other, but I guess our love wasn't strong enough to make one of us compromise. I knew that I was really going to miss her, but I guess it wasn't meant to be. I could have thought of every cliché, but what good would it do? Unfortunately, Josephine was in a tough situation, being in the middle between her family and me. In the long run, she chose her family over me, and I believe she made the wrong decision, but that is just my opinion. Wrong or not, the decision was made, and it wasn't to my favor. The last day in California, I tried one more time to get her to change her mind. You see, I am a very proud person, and I always did things with pride, but that last day with her, I got down on my knees and begged her to come back with me, but she declined.

Saying goodbye to someone you really love is not an easy thing to do, especially when it was the woman who was almost my wife. It was a very emotional day. We tried to ask why this relationship had to end like this. There was no easy answer. All we could do was concentrate on the wonderful time that we had had together; everything else was secondary. I put my arms around her and hugged and kissed her for the last time. My friend Steve drove me to the airport.

25

I had such mixed feelings. I was going home, but by the same token, I had lost a very special part of my life whom I loved very much. It was so close but so far...now I understood what that cliché meant. Steve and I had a drink at the airport, and he tried to console me. I thanked him for his sympathy, but told him only time will heal this wounded heart.

My plane arrived, and Steve and I said our goodbyes. The trip from California to Rhode Island took six hours, so I had plenty of time to reflect on the situation. I felt I did everything in my power to give Josephine a good life. I also knew that if her family hadn't interfered in our relationship, she and I would be coming back to Rhode Island as a married couple. It really hurt, especially because I loved her so much. I really couldn't explain it to anyone because I believed that if she really loved me, then we should have been married. That hurt. Maybe there was a remote possibility that our love wasn't deeply rooted enough to take that next step. Whatever the reason was, I was heading back to Rhode Island alone.

My brother Michael picked me up at the T.F. Green Airport. I took one look at him and started weeping. During the trip back to Bristol, we talked a lot; or I talked a lot, and he was a good listener. I felt like I had just lost my best friend, and I couldn't get her back. My brother was very understanding and very patient with me. I was a broken man, but my brother grabbed my hand and said, "Joseph, my brother, you will be alright. It might take some time, but in a while, you will overcome this situation just like you have overcome everything else in your life. You are a proven winner, and you will overcome this. A lot of people without a disability have not accomplished what you have accomplished with a disability. Joseph, you have something that many people don't have. You have a strong will that will never be broken, no matter what the circumstances are, and I am proud to be your brother."

We arrived home, and naturally, it was great to see my family, who were very supportive. There was a three-hour time difference between the East and West coasts. I wanted to call Josephine, but she was still at work. My mother objected to the telephone call because she really loved Josephine, but because of the way things turned out, she was very angry with her. I tried to convince my mother that it wasn't Josephine's fault; it was the circumstances that prevented us from getting married. According to my mother, I was still the baby in the family, even though I was the oldest. My brothers took me aside and told me that while I was in California, there wasn't a day that went by that my mother didn't talk about me. I really meant a lot to my mother, so I didn't push the issue about the phone call. Before I went to bed, I would just call Josephine to tell her that I had a good trip and arrived safely.

I called her at 11:00 p.m. Eastern time (8:00 p.m. Pacific time), and she answered the phone. It was great to hear her voice; it was only a few hours, but I really missed her greatly. Naturally, it was a very emotional conversation; all I wanted to do was to hold her one more time in my arms and just tell her that I loved her. Inside, I was tearing up because it seemed like my whole being was destroyed, because she was such a big part of my life. I have known a lot of wonderful women over the years, but no one like her. Unfortunately, the circumstances weren't going to allow us to be together. We finally hung up the telephone, and I went straight to my room. That night I couldn't sleep. Every time I tried to close my eyes, all I could see was her face. I think that was the longest night of my life. I was doubting myself and asking if I had made the right decision or the wrong one. This was the question that hung on for a few months, and I had to go through this alone.

When the two of us came out to Rhode Island at Christmas, my mother had poured her heart out to Josephine and told her how glad she was that her son had found someone to love and who loves him. My mother's dream was to find the perfect person for me, and my mother had seen the caring between Josephine and me. My mother loved her right away, and when she found out that Josephine had not come home with me to live, it really disturbed her. I found out later that whenever Josephine called me, my mother would tell her not to call anymore.

A couple of weeks passed, and I called Josephine one weekend. Once again, it was an emotional conversation for both of us. I told her how much I missed her, and she told me the same thing. Josephine also told me that maybe she made a mistake, and she would reconsider coming to Rhode Island, but she would need some time. I was very excited and asked her how much time she meant. She told me she would need two or three months because she wanted to slowly break away from her family. I said, "If you're serious about coming here, why wait two or three months? Why don't I just send you a plane ticket and come out tomorrow?"

She believed her way would be the better option. I was eager and happy when Josephine told me that I had to find a job and start to save for our future. I had not had good luck finding work, and all my resources were being drained. My brothers told me to go back to school and complete my degree. They were right, but I decided that if I found a job, I would go back to school at night. I landed a job as a shipping and receiving clerk in a retail store. I enjoyed it, but it didn't pay very much. I forgot about school and decided to take on a second job. I got a second job working for the Town of Bristol as an assistant to a youth group at a place where kids would go after school, rather than spending time on the streets. They were nice kids. They were very interested in cerebral palsy, and they would ask all types of questions. We had a lot of fun. They learned from me, and I learned from them.

In the meantime, Josephine and I would speak over the telephone to find out what was going on in each other's lives. Every time I talked to her, it seemed that our hearts were very distant from each other. I also understood that if this relationship was going to last, it would take a miracle from God. The letters were few and far between, and I knew deep down in my heart that this relationship could not last if it was only over the telephone or by letter. Something had to give because it wasn't fair to either one of us. I just wanted an answer one way or the other because I really wanted my life to go forward instead of standing still the way it was, and I wanted to establish myself in Rhode Island.

The retail business was slowing down, and the store manager, Mr. Casey, called me in. He said that business was slow, and he was going to have to cut my hours in half. I was disappointed because I really gave my best to that company. My other job was just part-time, and I couldn't get any more hours because it was budgeted by the town of Bristol. Two weeks later, Mr. Casey laid me off. He gave me a high grade for my performance, but the way business was going, he couldn't keep me on. I was, of course, disappointed, but I understood that it had to be done. I believe one of the reasons I got laid off was that I was physically limited to what I could and couldn't do. Even though I had the desire, unfortunately, once again, my body couldn't agree with my brain. That began to frustrate me once again because all I wanted was a chance to prove that I could be equal with others in society. I always was a proud individual—maybe too much at times—but I needed that to get me through the rough times.

In the meantime, I called Josephine and asked her what she wanted to do about our relationship. She said she wanted me to come back to California, get married to her, and live out there, but away from her family. I didn't really think she could break away from her family, and as much as we loved each other, we both prioritized our families over each other. Even though it hurt terribly, we broke it off. I did tell her that I would always be there for her, but as far as our relationship went, I didn't think it was fair to string each other along. I knew that when Josephine got married, her husband was going to be a fortunate man.

I knew it was time to move on with my life, and with the help and support of my parents, brothers, and friends, I couldn't fail. It was going to take time to get over Josephine, but I guess everyone who has broken up with someone they have loved must go through the process of healing, and I was no exception. There were times when I woke up with tears in my eyes. I could only imagine the life we could have had, but it wasn't meant to be.

The job with the town was winding down for the season. I started looking for work, but with no success. The more time you have on your hands, the more time you must just think. Naturally, I thought of Josephine and what I could have done to make our relationship work. I wasn't a quitter. I always gave my best. At times, it didn't work out, but I always tried. I knew that one day everything would fall into place, and if I kept plugging away, I would find what I was looking for. I have always had a strong will, and if my will hadn't been broken by this, it would never be broken.

Part Three

26

Communities had always been valuable to me, so I joined the Benevolent Protection of Elks. I admired that they supported charities, including United Cerebral Palsy. I got accepted, and everyone there was very nice to me and made me feel right at home. I was amazed because no matter where you come from and no matter what background you have, everyone is treated as equal. That word equal was a word that had been very seldom used in my life. I also felt like I counted. It was nice. They were very understanding because I was currently completely out of work, and they gave me moral support and offered to help me in any way they could.

I submitted my name to an organization called Projects With Industry (PWI). This was an organization that helped people with disabilities find jobs. I met a wonderful person by the name of Mike Bisillio, who took a special interest in me. He helped me with my resume, applications, etc. I called every day to find out what was going on that day. I felt bad because I pestered him every day, and there were other people with disabilities who were also looking for work. One day, he called and told me that something might be available, and he would get back to me. I found out later that the company that was interested in me had some questions about my employment history and why I couldn't hold on to a job. He suggested that they give me an interview and judge for themselves. I interviewed, and they told me they would get back to me. I called Mike and told him the interview lasted an hour and fifteen minutes. He said that was a good sign because interviews usually didn't last that long. The company was a law firm called Edwards & Angell. I found out later that I wasn't their first choice. At the time, the recession had hit Rhode Island, and there were a lot of people looking for work. They hired someone else first because this particular position required a lot of walking, and they took this person over me for that reason. This person went to lunch one day and never returned!

On August 29, 1989, I got hired as a messenger. I started right away and was extremely happy. My boss at the time, Alice Greene, did everything that she could to help my coworkers be comfortable with me, as Edwards & Angell had never hired anyone disabled before. To be honest with you, I really didn't know how my coworkers would adapt to me, but according to them, I was a smash hit.

Alice called me into her office one morning and told me that she had never worked with someone with my disability, so it would take time to find out what I could and couldn't do. With my stubbornness, I tried to do everything that my coworkers did because I felt that if I was getting paid like them, then I should work like them. The people there were very nice and made me feel right at home. Work was fun, plus I was enjoying the people around me.

Edwards & Angell never had a disabled employee, so this was a big accomplishment for both them and for me. A month went by, and the firm tried to hire another disabled person, but that person only lasted three weeks. Unfortunately, Edwards & Angell felt that because I was able to do certain tasks, other handicapped workers could do the same, but it didn't work out. It was an honor and a privilege that they thought I did such a good job that they would hire other handicapped people, but the fact was that I wasn't special; I was just too stubborn and sometimes too stupid to give up. At times, I didn't feel like I was disabled at all, and maybe, just maybe, if I wasn't acting disabled, they would realize that they could depend on me. Whatever the reason was, I was just happy because deep down inside I knew that I could perform on a par with my fellow coworkers. It was all made possible through that person who left at his lunch hour. If he had come back, I would never have been hired!

PWI was very happy with my accomplishments at Edwards & Angell. They wrote an article about me in the newsletter that they published once a month. They also had breakfast in my honor. I was amazed at myself for the accomplishments I had made. I knew that I had the ability, but it took PWI to give me a chance. All I needed was the opportunity to prove myself to the workforce. Now that I had it, it was up to me to really turn that chance into something special.

My coworkers also gave me the chance to really flourish, and they helped me in every way. I also believe that I made them appreciate life a little more and showed them not to take so many things for granted. The only thing I really couldn't do was to carry liquid, and I love my coffee. There was always someone around to make me a cup of coffee. Now I felt like a complete person, and I felt whole. The beauty of this was that I didn't go out of my way to do anything special; I was just myself. I was beginning to feel enjoyment in my life.

I kept involved with activities outside of work, but I felt like something was missing. I felt that I had to do something extraordinary again for United Cerebral Palsy. I knew that the Elks were a major contributor to UCP. In January of 1989, I began planning a walk from Bristol to Providence, a distance of 18.3 miles, and I planned to ask people to pledge money for every mile I walked. I spoke to a few Elks members about doing the walkathon, and they thought it was a great idea. Plus, it would get other people involved in fundraising and awareness. I was determined to do it, and with some help, I felt that I could get enough support. This could be one of the best fundraising activities I could ever do. The Elks participated every year in these telethons to raise money for Cerebral Palsy. In fact, ten percent of the money raised in RI for Cerebral Palsy came from the Elks.

My walk was on. I would walk from Bristol to Providence on January 22, 1990. I received all kinds of support from the Elks and from people outside of the lodge. The local paper featured an article about the walkathon on the front page. I was very proud of the task I was ready to accomplish. Donations kept pouring in. People I did not even know donated money because they felt compassion and wanted to support the project. On Saturday at 5:30 in the morning, Robert Sackett, David Sears, and I set out for the journey to Providence from Bristol. Even though it was winter, the weather was nice. We went through Warren, Barrington, East Providence, and Providence. It took eight and a half hours, and I was hurting when we got to the end! But I knelt down on the ground and kissed it. I didn't know if I would finish it, but thank God I did.

The next day, I was so sore I couldn't walk. I was scheduled to be on the United Cerebral Palsy telethon at 3:00 p.m. to talk about the walkathon. The three of us went on together and talked about the walk. Robert and Dave did most of the talking because I was hurting, so all I did was smile. While we walked, Robert was worried because I had never done this before, and he saw the pain that I was in. He asked if I wanted to quit, but I shouted, "No!" I was determined to finish what I said I was going to do. After Robert and David left the stage, the interviewer asked me to stay on stage for a one-on-one interview, and I agreed. Charlie Jeffers, a well-known radio announcer, interviewed me. He asked, "Joseph, what does cerebral palsy mean to you?" I smiled and told him that I was blessed with cerebral palsy. He looked rather shocked and asked me to explain what I meant. I told him that if I had been born physically normal, I would not be there that day. I had learned, I told him, that there was hope that there would be a better tomorrow. I couldn't believe these words were coming out of my mouth, especially since a few years before, I had been cursing Cerebral Palsy. Finally, I concluded by saying cerebral palsy enriched my life better than any physical body ever could, and that without it, I would not be half the man I was at that time.

I got home that evening and laid down, and I started to think about what I had just accomplished. Tears started flowing out of my eyes because I never thought that my life would wind up like that. This kind of thing could only happen in a Hollywood script, but instead it was my life unfolding before my own eyes. I could never imagine that things would ever turn out like this; it was too good to be true. Now I could really say that my life was truly blessed, and I could believe it.

That evening, I called Alice and told her that I didn't think I was going to come to work the next day. She told me that they all knew what I had just accomplished and to take a few days off and rest. Believe me, I rested and slept like a baby. The next morning, Edwards & Angell sent me flowers. I was shocked because I never thought I would get flowers from them. They were a very big law firm with offices in New York, Palm Beach, Boston, New Jersey, Connecticut, and Providence, and still took the time to send me flowers. Also, the phone would not stop ringing, and I finally had to take it off the hook.

After two days, I returned to work. The employees greeted me very nicely, and it made me feel very special. I really didn't think what I had done was such a big deal, because other people could have done it at a much faster pace. But someone told me that other people hadn't lined up to do it, and I should give myself credit. I was really happy that I had physically been able to do it. I realized I should just be proud of what I had accomplished, and I was, but deep down, I knew I had to do more, and with people's help, I was going to do a lot more.

27

I came up with a crazy notion about driving my own car. My parents disagreed, and my brothers thought it was a great idea. After explaining to my parents why I should get my driver's license, they disapproved but gave me their blessings. Because I was disabled, I had to go to a hospital to get tested. I passed all the tests with flying colors. In the meantime, my brother Victor was the only one who would let me drive his car. Michael and Thomas looked at me and said, "Joe, we love you very much, but you are not going to drive our cars." Victor was a more carefree-natured kind of guy, and his car was a bit older than those of my other brothers. Every day after work, he would pick me up and we would go for about an hour. He had a lot of patience with me and corrected me in a loving way if I made mistakes. I wanted to learn so much because I wanted to be independent, and without my license, I would always have to depend on someone to take me around. Even though people didn't mind taking me around, I felt like I was imposing on someone at some point or other. My goal was to get my license and get the freedom that I longed to have, but I had to work very hard in order to achieve my goal. I really didn't mind the hard work because in everything I did, if I wanted something, I had to work harder.

Even though I was practicing with Victor, I still had some doubts about my ability, but I would try my best all the time. Victor would grade me every day and keep a chart on how I was doing. There were days that I would do very well, and there were also days when I didn't do so well. To tell the truth, I was scared, but this was something I had to do.

I received a telephone call from Rhode Island Hospital to come in and get tested to see if I had the physical ability to drive. That was the first step to achieving my goal; next was the bigger challenge: the road test. The hospital recommended that I need at least fifteen hours of instruction on the road. There was a person named Mr. Polumbo, who specialized strictly in working with physically disabled people. He owned his own company. He asked why I wanted to drive. I told him I wanted to achieve complete independence for myself. He said he couldn't promise me that, but if determination had anything to do with it, I was on my way. He let me drive for about half an hour, and I was so excited I was like a kid in a candy store. We returned to my driveway, and he told me he would get in touch with me in a couple of weeks, and we would work out a schedule.

A couple of weeks went by, and Mr. Polumbo called me at work and asked if my boss was willing to let me go for about an hour once a week. I talked to Alice and explained the situation, and we arranged for me to take time off on Wednesdays at 3:00 p.m. I was so excited that I couldn't think straight. After work, I went home and explained to my parents that Mr. Polumbo would be giving me driving lessons.

They were worried, but I told them this was something I had to do. No matter what I said, my parents wouldn't change their minds. I loved them, but I was determined to do this. When the time came, I met Mr. Polumbo in the parking lot. I was looking for his car, and when I found it, I realized his license plate said, "U CAN 2." Looking at that license plate gave me tremendous confidence that I could do anything, even conquer the world.

In the meantime, a new position opened up in the accounting department at work, and I applied for it. A few days later, I got a call from human resources and was told that they wanted to meet with me after I got through work. I thought I got the position, and I was very excited. But that wasn't the case; I came in second. Another person who had recently graduated from Rhode Island College had gotten the job. I wasn't that disappointed; however, because I would have done the same thing—taken the person with the higher education. The person in the human resources office said, "Joseph, it came down to the two of you, and you guys were so equal we had to go with the person with the higher education, because the two of you were equal on every other count." I looked at her and asked her to repeat the sentence. When she repeated the word equal, I stopped her. I told her that no one had ever said I was equal to someone else before, and it was wonderful to hear that. I told her that they had made the right decision, and that just to be "equal," I felt I had gotten the position too.

This made me realize that if I wanted to advance, I needed to go back to school and finish my degree. I contacted the school I had attended eight years before, Johnson & Wales. I found out that in the eight years since I had been there, they had become a university. I explained to them that I was a student there before and had graduated in 1983 with an associate's degree. They couldn't find any records on me, so they asked me to come and see if they could clear this up. I told Alice that I would be late, but I needed to handle this issue.

When I got there, everything had changed around. I had a tough time finding everything because the school had grown so much since I had been there. After some time, they still couldn't find my records, so I tried to identify some professors I had in the past. They let me register to take some classes. I decided to take two, because I didn't want to overdo it at first. I signed up for Sociology and Western Civilization and picked up my books. I was two hours late getting back to work, and Alice was fine with my explanation. I insisted that I would make up the time. As I got older, I learned that honesty really is the best policy.

I got home and I needed to spend some time alone, and it dawned on me that the week was pretty much filled up, and I didn't have any free time for myself. I realized I really didn't care. I just wanted to do the best that I could do and felt that everything else would just fall into place. I had registered to go back to college and was really looking forward to it. Thankfully, the school called and told me that they had found my records! I asked them how my records had been lost in the first place, and they said the school had transposed my Social Security number. I thought it was amazing that a few numbers here and a few numbers there could make it seem like a person had disappeared from the face of the earth. But I was like a bad penny: I kept coming back. I had too much to live for, and a transposed number was not going to wipe me out.

It seemed like everything was happening very quickly, and that was the way I liked it, because I didn't think of Josephine when I was so busy. When I did think about her, I would mope around for a couple of days, so I tried to stay occupied. On special occasions, especially holidays, it was tough. Somehow, I got through it, but it still hurt inside. I tried desperately not to show it, but those who really knew me could see right through me. I had to remain busy, no matter how large or small the task—I just wanted to stay busy.

People were concerned about the fact that I was taking on so much and was always on the go. I used to tell them not to worry about it because that was the kind of person I was. In reality, I was hurting inside more than people could imagine. Staying busy helped me so that I didn't have to think about my personal life. I was content just helping people whenever they needed my help. I couldn't say no because it wasn't in my vocabulary.

My driving was going pretty well, but Mr. Polumbo noticed that every now and then, I would swerve the car to the left or right for two or three seconds. That was due to my condition; sometimes I would have a muscle spasm. I tried to work on it, and it was hard, especially because I was born with it. I never took medication because I didn't believe in it, and I didn't want to depend on it. I was pretty stubborn when it came to taking medications. When I got a headache, my last option was to take aspirin. I tried to stay away from medication for as long as I could. Mr. Polumbo told me that I was basically doing pretty well and that the swerving was the only flaw.

28

My mother and I had always had a good line of communication. One day, I came in from work, and she looked at me and smiled. I asked her what was so funny, and in her loving way, she put her arms around me and said, "Joe, look at yourself then, and look at yourself now." I told her it was only going to get better. She told me she knew. Love from a mother is something that every human being should experience in a lifetime. There is no feeling in the world better than a mother's true love.

On Tuesdays and Thursdays, instead of going home, I would stop and get a bite to eat and then study before class. Then, at 6:00 p.m., I would go to class. Surprisingly enough, I was doing pretty well. I made a lot of friends in college, and they all respected me for who I was. In fact, one student thanked me for coming into his life because he drew strength from me. I was in total amazement when he told me this. I did ask him to explain, and he simply said, "Joe, before I met you, I took everything at face value. Now I just take a moment every day to count my blessings." That was something I did not expect to hear, and tears flowed down my face.

When I was in class, I had a tough time taking notes, so the professor allowed me to use a tape recorder. However, that was tough because after I taped the class, I had to go home and listen to the whole class again. It seemed like I was doubling my effort by listening to the class twice—it was bad enough that the class was four hours long! There was a student named Ana Rebello who sat next to me. One day, I explained to her about using the tape recorder instead of taking notes, and what a pain that was. She told me she had noticed that I was having a tough time with the notes. She asked for my fax number at work and told me to just listen to the professor. The next day, I went to work and did my normal everyday tasks. I got a call from the people who handled the fax machine saying I had a fax waiting for me. Curious, I went to get it, because I had no idea who would send me a fax. It was from Ana, the student who sat next to me. She had sent me her notes from class. I was totally shocked that someone would take the time to do that. I called her to thank her, but she told me I had already thanked her just by being myself.

Classes ran from 6:00 p.m. to 9:45 p.m., and I lived in Bristol. The bus from Providence to Bristol left at 9:30 p.m. My brothers would pick me up, but that really was an inconvenience for them, and even though they never complained, it bothered me. I lied to them and told them I had a ride home from school, so I wouldn't need their services. In truth, I waited for the next (and last) bus that came at 11:05. If I missed that, I would call a taxi or get a hotel room for the night.

I found out one day that James Alves, the guidance counselor I had in seventh grade, was teaching at Johnson & Wales. I knew it would be great to see him, and when I did, he gave me a big hug. I said, "What are you doing here?" and he said, "I can't ever get rid of you, can I?" and laughed. He was now a principal at another school and was teaching Psychology 101 on Tuesday evenings. He asked me if I needed a ride home. It was a blessing because at least I didn't have to wait for the bus. On the way home, we talked about many things, and he told me, "Joseph, you have been a blessing in my life." I said, "You know, Mr. Alves, everyone tells me that I am a blessing, or they thank me for coming into their lives." He said, "Only a fool wouldn't notice the kind of person that you are. You were born disabled, so you could teach people like me how to live life." I was stunned when he said that, because I had always thought that I'd been born with a strike against me, but he told me that every time I got up to bat in the game of life, I hit a home run.

It had taken me a long time to admit this, but I had come to believe that being born with cerebral palsy was the best thing that could ever have happened to me. Don't get me wrong, if I had a choice, I would have taken a physically normal body any day. However, when I put everything in perspective, I have come to realize that being born with CP has allowed me to reach people in a special way. I also believe that if I were born like most people, I would not have the same outlook that I have today. I have to believe this because if I believe that God is running the whole show, and if he doesn't treat everyone equally, then I feel cheated. It took me a long time to get out of the hole that I was in. I choose to believe that CP is a blessing instead of a curse. Again, people may differ with me, and they are entitled to their personal opinion, and I respect that, but I would rather believe my opinion than theirs because it works for me. I have been truly blessed because I have reaped a lot of rewards through my CP. Oscar Wilde said, "What seems to us bitter trials are often blessings in disguise." When I hear people say the kind of things that Mr. Alves said to me, I feel humbled, but at the same time, it gives me confidence to keep going.

One Thursday evening, I was stuck for a ride, and Mr. Alves happened to come in that evening for a meeting. He saw me studying and asked why I was still there. I told him I didn't have a ride home on Thursday evening, and was waiting for the late bus, so I was passing the time by studying. He asked me to wait for him, and he would take me home after his meeting. The next Tuesday, I went to class, and Mr. Alves met me at the break. He introduced me to a new student, Alan Merrit, who became my new ride to Bristol. He was a little older than I was and had the same major. That meant that he was going to take pretty much the same classes I was taking, which meant I had a ride home. Alan introduced me to one of his friends, Chris Ricci. I liked him right away because he was like me, except that he was physically normal. He was also a management major. We three became very good friends both in and out of school. We studied together, and our friendship grew strong over time. Alan and Chris were both married and enjoyed going out together with their wives. They often invited me to come along. I wasn't seeing anyone at the time, and I felt like a third wheel—in this case, a fifth wheel. So, when they got together, I found something else to do on my own.

29

The Elks had a Las Vegas weekend as a fundraiser for United Cerebral Palsy, and I asked my boss, Alice, if she'd like to attend. She said yes and drove me home from work so I could change my clothes. She met my parents, who were naturally very grateful to her for giving me an opportunity to have a job. They loved her right away and told her that, thanks to her, new avenues had opened for me. They said they always knew I had the ability, but they thought I would need someone to help me get my foot in the door, and they said Alice was that person.

We got to the Elks, and we ordered a drink, and my cribbage partner Harry showed up. He and I were partners for Wednesday night cribbage, and we were pretty good. I introduced Harry to Alice, and we sat down to play poker. I was losing, but I really didn't care, because all the proceeds were going to UCP of Rhode Island. As the night went on, I started to win. By the time the night wound down, I had won about seventy dollars. I cashed in my chips and donated my money to UCP. It wasn't much, but it was going to a good cause. I vowed to myself before I died that I would like to see the words cerebral palsy abolished from the dictionary. I know that would be a tall order, but with a lot of research and hope, maybe I will see it; it is my life's goal to achieve. I looked at my nephews and thanked god that they were born healthy. Everyone should have the good fortune to be born healthy.

United Cerebral Palsy called me on a regular basis, asking if I would do lectures to parents with CP and to the public, and I could not say no. If I didn't have time, somehow, I would make the time. I was often physically and mentally exhausted, but what could I do? I didn't have much of a personal life, other than when I hung out with my best friend, Gary Grifka. Gary and I met through a cup of coffee in a coffee shop, and our friendship has grown each passing day. Even though I have three brothers that God blessed me with, Gary was like a breath of fresh air. There isn't anything I wouldn't do for him.

Alice wanted to talk with me and offered to take me to lunch. At lunch, she told me that she was interested in Harry. It was funny because at cribbage, Harry had inquired about Alice. It was easy to set up their first "date." We made plans to go to cribbage on a Wednesday night. I had planned to go too as a buffer, but unfortunately, it snowed like crazy that night, and cribbage was canceled. We three relented and decided to go get a drink. I left them at a table and sat at the bar so they could get to know each other. We left after two hours, and they had made a date for the following Saturday.

I had been thinking about Josephine, and deep down in my heart, I knew our relationship would stay distant, and that was sad to me. I was always an optimist, but I had to face the reality that we would never again make eye contact. That would be something that would haunt me for a while, especially with Valentine's Day just around the corner. We always did something special on that very special day. This year, it hit me like a ton of bricks that it was going to be different from the last two years, because I was never going to see her again. This was something I was going to have a tough time swallowing.

I was never a quitter, but if I was going to have peace within myself, I was going to have to deal with this situation. I had started to date other women, and I felt that it wasn't fair for me to do that.

I had to confront the situation once and for all. I called her one day, and she answered the phone. I had written down everything I wanted to say, but instead, I spoke with my heart, and I told her what my heart wanted her to hear. I told her our relationship wasn't meant to be. I thanked her for being such a wonderful, loving person. When I told her, I felt we had to carry on life without each other. We both started to cry. Her birthday (June 20) was coming up, and I had always sent her a present, but I told her that this year I was not going to send her anything. At the end of our conversation, I said goodbye and asked her to please not call anymore unless it was a life-or-death situation. I knew that was harsh, but I needed to carry on with my life. Deep down, I think both of us knew it was over, but neither one of us wanted to admit it. I think I had to do it. After I hung up, I got the waste basket and started to clean up everything that I had of her and threw it away. It was tough, but it had to be done. If I had waited another day, I don't think I'd have had the heart to do it. I went to bed and couldn't sleep. I tossed and turned, and every time I closed my eyes, all I could see was her face. I think I finally fell asleep around 3:00 a.m.

The next day I got up, exhausted, but I went to work. I was hoping that the day would go by fast because I had class that evening. I didn't want it to be one of the longest nights I had experienced in my life. Work went fine because I was used to what I had to do. But that particular evening, I had an exam that I had forgotten to study for the previous evening. I was the last person to leave the room.

30

The next week, the professor wanted to speak with me and asked if everything was all right. I hadn't done very well on the exam. I explained to him what had happened, and he said he would give me a makeup test. I told him that I knew I could have done a lot better if I had studied like I normally did, and that I didn't feel it was fair to ask him to spend his weekend making a new test for me when it was my own fault. He was astonished at my answer, because most students would jump at the opportunity to take a make-up. But I wasn't sick; it was my own stupid fault. The professor had told the class that he would drop the lowest grade. I told him that if he hadn't said that, I would have taken the makeup, but since he was going to do that, I would guarantee that this would be my lowest grade. I asked him what my actual grade was, and he said, "Joe, you don't want to know!" I really didn't want to know because if he said that, it must be pretty bad, but I was curious because I wanted to know where to study next time. He couldn't say it, but he wrote it down, and even I was shocked, because I usually received a pretty good mark. It was a forty. I told him to mark this day down because I promised him he would never see that grade on my work again.

Some people don't have to study that much and are still

able to get good grades. My brother, Thomas, is like that, and I'm a little envious that all they have to do is look over their notes and get a good grade. I tried to do that, and the result was a forty, so that told me that in order to get good grades, I had to study and really work at it. When I took my studies seriously, it paid off. It was tough, especially on the weekend when my brothers got together and tried to do something. I usually didn't participate because I was studying.

When I went back to school, I applied for financial aid and received a Pell Grant. I think I was awarded $1,490.00. A few weeks went by, and they took it back because I was a full-time employee. When I started at Edwards & Angell, I wasn't making what everyone else was making. Thank God I was living with my parents, because I would not have been able to survive on my own. I really didn't want to drop out, so I took out a student loan for $4000 that covered the first year.

I was disappointed and angry because here I was, a disabled person, and couldn't get any financial help for bettering myself. That really didn't make sense to me because there are a lot of people who are physically able to work and still try to take advantage of the system. That really bothered me to no end. Legally, true, I was physically disabled, but that was where the disability stopped. I was a handicapped person who fell through the cracks. Disabled, yes, but in order to succeed, I had to work like a physically able person would work. It's a lot of hard work, which I can appreciate, but it's harder when you have the physical limitations of a disability. I have since learned through the years that there are a lot of handicapped people in the same boat. Disabled, but not disabled enough to qualify for any benefits that other people could get.

Projects With Industry contacted me because I had been chosen to receive an award. It was their first annual dinner, and I was to be awarded the first-ever community service award for 1991. I was very excited because I had put in a lot of hard work over the years, and now, I was being recognized. Plus, to be the first to receive the award was a great honor. The guest speaker was Patrick Kennedy, a State Representative from Rhode Island, one of a long line of public servants from the Kennedy Family. When my firm found out that I was receiving the award, they bought ten tickets and reserved a table. Patrick Kennedy spoke on the Americans with Disabilities Act (ADA) and the small percentage of the workforce that was disabled. It was then and there that I became proud of being disabled because I was proud of being an American at work.

When Mike Bisillio introduced me as the first person to win the award, I was very nervous. I went up to receive the award, and they asked me to say a few words. First, I thanked Carmen, Michael, Michelle, and Mary, the people who made up Project With Industry at that time, for selecting me for the award. Secondly, I thanked Edwards & Angell for believing in me when most companies would not even give me a job interview. Then I spoke a little bit about myself and living with my disabilities. It wasn't easy, but through hard work, it had finally begun to pay off. In conclusion, I said that, disabled or not, there were three words that measure the successful person: desire, determination, and courage. Now, no one can give this to you; you must want it in order to achieve your goals and dreams.

When I got home, my parents were still up, and I showed them the award. They were very proud of me. I wanted them to be there because if it wasn't for their patience and heartache, I wouldn't be here today. My mother reminded me that they didn't speak English and would not have understood what was going on. She also said that they had always known I would be successful; it was just a matter of time. I kissed them and went to my room. I got undressed and I started weeping; not tears of sorrow but tears of joy. I thought about the past, and I realized that being disabled was the best thing that ever happened to me. I realized that I had a lot of work ahead of me if I was going to impact the handicapped community. A lot of work and involvement had to be done, and with God's grace, it would be done.

The next morning, I went to work, and the marketing department wanted to do a feature on me for their newsletter. Again, I was honored, and it reinforced the pride that had been growing within my heart. I was pretty excited to be working for the largest law firm in Rhode Island. I always thought that working for a firm this big, you would become just a number or get lost in the shuffle, but I was wrong. Besides, I'm pretty easy to find—just look for the guy with the limp. Not that I was complaining. Now it was time to count my blessings, each and every one of them.

Wednesday rolled along, and it was time for my driving lessons with Mr. Polumbo. I was excited every time I was behind the wheel. First, we went to the highway, and I did pretty well. Then we came to the city, and I started to become nervous. I noticed that with cars and people around me, I got very frustrated. Mr. Polumbo was a wonderful man. He tried to make me relax by telling jokes and trying to make me loosen up, but it was no use; I just became more nervous. At the end of my lesson, he told me to practice with my brother because he thought it would help with this problem. Other than that, he said I was doing fine. My brother Victor would take me out, and he told me the same things, but I would still get pretty upset and frustrated. My mind would want to drive, but my body would not cooperate. I was trapped between body and mind.

I developed a passion for writing, so that evening when I got home, I went into my room and began to write. I started with the word "battle," and the words kept flowing onto the pad. I wrote a story about cerebral palsy. I called it The Ultimate Battle. It goes as follows:

The Ultimate Battle

There is a constant battle that goes on with my body. It is between my body and my brain. You see, both of them are stubborn and each wants their own space to shine, and neither of them will give an inch, so I can live a peaceful life. They would rather continually battle with themselves. Both of them know that neither one can win, but they would rather fight than come up with a peaceful solution.

You see, my brain tells my body to do a particular task, and my brain responds by saying, "I can't do it. Please find another solution to complete the task." The trouble begins when the brain cannot find another solution because my brain is geared for a normal physical body, rather than for a physically disabled body. My brain cannot understand this, so it continuously feeds the same information without compromises in sight.

There will never be a clear-cut winner. Sometimes the brain wins, other times the body wins, but they are so close that there is never a clear-cut winner. The sad part is that I will never experience complete harmony between my brain and my body. Only towards the end of my life will one of them realize that they were wrong, but by that time, it will be too late because that is when my life will come to an end. That is too bad because just once, I would have loved to have complete cooperation between my brain and my body. That is wishful thinking, I know, because that's something where they can't reach a compromise.

I can only hope and pray that one day the brain and body can live in perfect harmony.

Honestly, pride in oneself builds character, and character is an intangible that sets people apart from one another. I was always set apart from the rest of the people around me, whether it was physically or not. No matter where I went, people always told me that I lit up a room. That made me think that, through my disability, it was up to me to do something positive. Every one of us has some kind of hidden talent, but how we choose to display that talent is entirely up to us. Either positive or negative, it's up to the individual to choose how they want to portray themselves.

Mr. Polumbo called me on the telephone and wanted to see me. I pretty much knew what he wanted to talk to me about. I met him after work, and he wanted to buy me a cup of coffee. I drove from Providence to Bristol. We went to a local coffee shop, and we started talking. He said, "Joe, your fifteen hours of driving school are up, and for the most part, you did pretty well. However, there were a few times when, because of your cerebral palsy, you lost control of the car. Now, I believe you can drive, but what will happen if you get into an accident because of your disability?" I looked at him and said, "Mr. Polumbo, you are totally right," and I started crying. I told him that without my driver's license, I would never experience complete independence, because no matter where I go, I will always have to depend on someone to take me around. I also told him that he was right, but before I left this earth, I would have my driver's license. He looked at me and smiled and said, "Joe, I don't doubt it. It might take you longer, but you will get it." He said he wasn't a betting man, but he would never bet against me. Then I tried to convince him that I could pass my road test, and maybe I could just carry my license with me and not drive. He said, "Joe, you could probably pass the road test and get your license, but if you had a license, you would be tempted and legally able to get a car down the road. I cannot recommend that." I shook my head and told him that he was right. As much as I didn't want to admit it to myself, he was right. I thanked him for the time and patience he had with me. He insisted the pleasure was all his.

When he left, I was pretty upset, so I went for a drink in the local pub. I started to think what more I could do to be happy, and I ordered another drink. All of a sudden, I realized what I was doing; every time things didn't go right, I tried to hide behind a drink. That was fine; however, why would I consume much more than what my body could handle? It just seemed strange; when things went well, I drank to socialize. But when things didn't go quite according to plan, I started to hide myself in a bottle. I asked myself a very important question. Basically, the question was "Joseph, have you really accepted your disability?" The answer was yes, but not really. I think I had accepted it about ninety-five percent of the way, but there was five percent of me that still was not accepting it. We as human beings are always concentrating on that five percent when we should be concentrating on the ninety-five percent in order to achieve happiness in our lives. Too many times, we try to portray someone that we are not. If you ask someone who they would rather be, they will say someone else, when they should say, "I'm happy with myself." No matter where we go on God's green earth, we can never find anyone quite like ourselves. You and I should be happy with ourselves and not be someone that we cannot be and won't be.

31

I had established myself as a pretty good worker, and my coworkers accepted me with open arms. It's funny, if you stay within your values and beliefs, you will be amazed at what you can accomplish with a little effort, honesty, and integrity. With those three words, if you apply them to your lives, there is no end to your success. However, we as human beings are lazy and want everything given to us on a silver platter. Unfortunately, life doesn't work that way. To be successful, we need to really establish a positive outlook towards life, and then we must establish goals in our lives. Whether short-term or long-term, we must have a target we are aiming for. Once you have achieved your goals, you need to establish new goals and objectives to reach for. This constant process goes on with us and life. Lest we forget that death will ultimately win in the end, in the meantime, we must win the little battles that life brings every day. We must also ensure that we have a sense of trust in our relationships, whether with family, friends, or coworkers. No matter how much we know and have, somewhere there is someone who can teach and influence us.

Our grades came out for the first trimester at Johnson & Wales, and I had a B average. I was pleased because with work and school, I had done pretty well. I knew I would have to work harder to maintain that B average, and if I wanted an A average, I would have to work even harder. All in all, I was pretty happy with my effort, especially because I had achieved it after an eight-year break from school.

Everything was going great, but I still felt like something was missing. I called the United Cerebral Palsy (UCP) of Rhode Island and expressed to them that I wanted to start a support group. They agreed because there was a support group in the West Bay area, but nothing in the East Bay area, so it was a perfect opportunity to start one. UCP helped me get started by calling people in the area, and I got some people to attend. It was great to see people wheeling themselves without complaining. I was totally humbled and thankful when I looked at them, and I knew I did not even have the right to gripe. For the first time, I really understood what the word humility meant. There were three people who attended the first meeting: Roseanne, Terri Ann, and Billy. When I saw them for the first time, I immediately adopted them as my brothers and sisters. They really exemplified how life should be lived to the fullest.

The group was formed to support and comfort each other. We discussed just about anything, and even I opened up about key issues—issues that I couldn't discuss with anyone. This support group was a release valve for my life, because I was speaking with handicapped people. I was supposed to be the leader of this group, and I experienced what joy and peace really meant. I really believe that my life came full circle when I started that support group because even though I wasn't physically normal, I wasn't really physically disabled either. I was really blessed with those three people in the group. It was also a source of strength for me, especially when I needed it. All I had to do was think about them, and it would bring up a smile.

People would come up to me to thank me for coming into their lives; however, I told them that my life was enriched more when I started the support group. People should be thanking the other members of the support group because they were teaching the real lesson that needed to be learned. Things that you and I take for granted, they have to struggle with.

My friends, Alice and Harry, got engaged to be married. Harry asked me if I wanted to be his best man. I thought it was a great honor, and I accepted with pleasure. Harry and Alice thought that since I was responsible for their relationship, it would be complete if I were the best man. I said, "You don't want a stag party, do you?" He didn't, so I got together some of his friends and some of mine and we took him out to dinner. A couple of months later, on December 1, 1991, they got married. A funny thing is: I had bought a new suit for the wedding, and the day that Harry got married, he picked me up and he was wearing the same suit! I looked at him and laughed and told him that this marriage was meant to be. I was happy they got married because it was wonderful that two people became one, and I was happy to be a part of that.

School was going great. Friends helped me in every way possible. I looked within and started to think how blessed I really was. At the same time, I wondered if I weren't disabled, would I be this popular with my peers? I really believe I would not have been, at that moment in time. I realized how my disability impacted people around me. It was truly a remarkable experience to go through, and I finally realized how my disability would touch people without me even trying. This helped me appreciate myself more because I now knew that my life was really a wonderful miracle. A miracle that, as a child, I thought would never materialize. Someone once said that if you find one good friend, consider yourself lucky. Well then, I have to be the most blessed man in the world because I have more than just one friend. I really believe that I am rich beyond measure in that respect.

I started to think that my life was turning around for the better. If we are patient with ourselves, then everything will fall into place. If I had been impatient, I might have missed connecting with all of these people. In life, we are dealt hands that we just don't like, and often we discard those cards instead of keeping them and playing them out. Maybe just that particular hand is the best hand for you for that particular situation, and who knows? Maybe you could be throwing away a winning hand. Always stay in the game, and never throw away your hand.

It is amazing how my life turned around, but I always had it in me—I just needed to be patient, but patience was never my strong suit. Sooner or later, I learned whatever lesson I was supposed to learn, I always did it the hard way. Now I just wanted to be the person that God intended for me to be, and I was going to try to the best of my ability. One thing I tried to do was take on too much responsibility, and it cost me. I noticed my mood swings, and people weren't accustomed to seeing that. Deep down, I wanted to make up for the years that almost ruined me. I really wanted to stay busy, even at work. If there was overtime, I would always be the one who asked for it first. My boss would tell me, "Joe, you are doing too much." Deep down, I was really hurting. I couldn't put my finger on it, but I knew something was missing. I tried many times to deal with it, I participated in the support group, but something was still missing inside, and it hurt when I was alone.

Then a few weeks went by, and I got a telephone call from Josephine. I knew right then and there what was missing. It was a companion, someone just to do things with. I answered the telephone, and it felt good talking to her. By the same token, I felt bad because it brought up a lot of conflicting feelings; feelings that were out of reach and out of control. Even though it was nice to hear her voice, I wished she hadn't called. One thing I was happy with was that we really didn't talk about the past. If you truly care about someone, you don't forget them, plus I didn't have anyone to fill that void. I had a lot of dates, but the ladies just weren't "the one." Usually, I'm a good judge of character, and I knew that because I was disabled, it would take a very special woman to have a relationship with me. As I got older, I thought of these things. Don't get me wrong; I knew in my heart that someday I would make a good husband and father, especially when I knew that my children would be born physically normal. I had doubts, and I didn't want to deprive any woman of anything, especially of a relationship.

My brother Michael and his wife Maria already had a son they had named Michael. God blessed them with another child, another boy. Mike picked me up and took me to the hospital to visit his wife. When I got there, I kissed Maria, but I was so excited about the baby that I didn't ask what the baby's name was. She gave me the birth certificate, and it read: Timothy Joseph Ferreira. I was in my glory to have a nephew named after me. That was a wonderful thing that they did.

In the meantime, my brother Thomas was planning on getting married. One night, he picked me up and took me for a ride. We were talking about how proud he was of me and all the things I had accomplished. I am a pretty emotional person, and I started to cry. He told me that he was proud to have a brother like me. He asked me a question that totally blew my mind. He said, "Joe, would you be my best man at my wedding?" I was shocked because I never expected him to ask that. I told him that it would be an honor and a privilege to be at his side on his wedding day. I also told him that if it wasn't for him, Michael, and Victor, I wouldn't be the person that I am. He looked at me and said, "When are you going to give yourself credit? It was you who did everything on your own!" He pointed out that not many people go from one coast to the other without knowing a soul, never mind a disabled person. But I had done that. I said, "Okay, I did it on my own, but you guys pushed me to go past my limitations."

When he dropped me off, I told him that God couldn't have given anyone three brothers better than the three he gave me. He said that I had enriched their lives even more. I said it then, and I will say it over and over until the day I die: God couldn't make better brothers for me. Each one of them had their own style, but all of their styles complement mine. We were all different, but when we all got together, it was a very special thing. All four of us had our own personal lives, yet we were always there for one another. I believe that is what makes our relationships so special. We have always been there to help each other whenever we needed each other. I keep on boasting about my brothers, but I can't help it because they are the ones who gave me physical and mental strength.

32

In January 1992, the recession hit the firm hard, and there were going to be layoffs. I believed that I was going to be one of the first to get my notice. In the past, when companies let go of personnel, I was usually one to go. To my amazement, Edwards & Angell kept me working. I was totally shocked and utterly surprised, because in ninety-nine years in the company's existence, they had never had a layoff. This time, due to the recession, they didn't have a choice. About forty people got their notices, and it was tough, especially when I worked with them, but it had to be done. I survived, which told me something: I was doing something right. Plus, every day since I got hired, I tried very hard to enjoy what I was doing, and I knew that I was contributing to the company's growth and productivity.

Each day that went by, I counted my blessings, because for the first time, I didn't feel like life's scapegoat like I had before. Edwards & Angell preached about equality, but now they had proven it, and I would be forever grateful. No matter what happened, Edwards & Angell believed I was a good worker and decided to keep me. I knew all along that I was a good employee, but it always seemed like I had gotten the short end of the stick. This time, there was finally an employer who believed in me enough to keep me, and I was very thankful. This is what helped me develop a more confident attitude about my abilities. I also felt like no matter what happened, I could develop into something special, thanks to the way I was treated at Edwards & Angell. True, I think in the beginning I was a project, but they saw something within me that I brought to the company that no one else had. I always knew that I had the ability, but it was especially rewarding to see a company have enough faith in me, and not many companies had shown that faith in the past. From then on, I vowed to myself that I would do what the company asked of me, and beyond. The company proved something to me by keeping me working. Now it was time to try to do all that I could to prove to them that I was worth the risk. They showed their confidence in me, and now it was time to show I had confidence in the company.

My support group was going great. We talked about life issues that affected a handicapped person on a daily basis. One of the topics we always talked about was self-respect. True, they didn't really have a choice in the way they were born. Still, it was a constant struggle for them just to motivate themselves. I told them with tears in my eyes, "Believe it or not, you guys are my motivation every day. I don't know why you were born like this, but for whatever reason, it shows people like me how to enjoy life to the fullest every day. You really have shown and taught me the true meaning of the word life." From that point on, it seemed as though they began to develop a higher sense of self-esteem. They were truly wonderful inspirations for people to count their wonderful blessings every day, one by one. These people were very special to me, and I told them that every time I saw them. I decided that whenever they needed me, I would be there for them. That was my pledge to them. I wanted them to feel that they could depend on me. I also assured them that no matter where they went, in my heart, I was always with them, and they should never worry because I would try to do whatever I could to make their lives easier.

One Saturday, we met and talked about the importance of friendship and how we develop bonds that turn into friendships. They asked me who had been my best friend in my lifetime. I told them that it was my mother. Over the years, my mother has been very important to me. I really feel that at times I deprived her of a life, because she put me ahead of everyone else, including herself. In a sense, she was my hero. If I had to pick someone to be my hero, it would have to be her. Everyone had the chance to express their feelings on this. Billy went last, and his answer blew my mind. He said, "My best friend is my Wheelchair." I asked him why, and he said, "Without my Wheelchair, I can't get anywhere, and I have to depend on someone to get me around."

Things seemed like they couldn't go any better for me. I felt like I was sitting on top of the world. I received my grades, and I finally made the Dean's List. I was very excited. I cherished the friendships I developed. People were very sensitive to my every need. It's amazing because if I had continued my education years earlier, when I graduated with a Bachelor of Science degree, then I would have missed out on these wonderful friendships that I made during this time. People came up to me thanking me for coming into their lives. To be honest with you, I was the lucky one, and really the blessed one, because without God, my family, and the friendships that I made over the years, I wouldn't be here writing this story. I was really blessed over the years, and now I was more thankful than ever before. I finally reached that mountain, and I intended to stay at the top. The family and friends that I had were going to make sure that I stayed there.

March 15, 1993, I laid my eyes upon a woman. I was completely overwhelmed by her. The building where I worked went smoke-free, so if you wanted to smoke, you had to go outside. As I was having my cigarette, I saw her and was completely consumed by her. You see, she walked with a cane, so automatically, there was a commonality between us. Being disabled and watching her walk with that cane, I was attracted to her. I went up to her and introduced myself, and we started to talk. Her name was Victoria Singer, and I liked her right away. You see, when I like someone, I usually go to extremes to get to know them. Every day, I waited for the exact time for her break and was right there waiting to greet her when she came out.

The strange thing was, the first time I laid my eyes upon her, I went home and wrote a poem about her. My company had given me a personal computer to use for school reports and term papers, because they knew that I had trouble writing. Edwards & Angell really took very good care of me. Even though I was disabled, my company was going to make sure that I was able to compete with the average person. I found that amazing because, sometimes, in business, people are often so busy with the competition that they forget about the people who work with them. But not Edwards & Angell; they gave me a competitive edge.

But I digress. Getting back to Victoria: that night, I wrote a story about her. When I write, I usually think about what I am going to write, but that particular night, I went home, and the words came up, jumping into my head. The story goes like this: I called it 'Miracle Eyes'.

Miracle Eyes

> I looked into her eyes, and my life hasn't been the same. It's a feeling that happens once in a lifetime. A feeling with such power that it cannot be

described. People have talked about this feeling, but I thought it never existed until I looked into her eyes.

When I looked at her, I saw the pain that she had gone through. She had an unselfish way about her; she didn't care about herself as much as she cared about others. She would much rather elevate others than elevate herself.

Her eyes told me so much about myself; more than I could ever realize in a lifetime. What she gave me, I could never repay in ten thousand lifetimes. Without her, I would not understand what life is. All my life, I have been praying for a miracle. The miracle happened when I looked into her eyes. When I think about it, I start to quiver; my whole insides turn into something that I can't even express. I get completely high when I look into her eyes. It's a high you cannot buy in any store or on any street corner. This high takes the place of any anger I ever felt. Her eyes expressed peace, joy, and giving of self for the benefit of others.

I just hope and pray that I can take the pain away from her because someone has done her wrong. In a strange way, it happened so that I could experience my miracle, a miracle that I never thought existed until I looked into her eyes. You see, I was born with a disability, and all my life I have been searching for a miracle, a miracle that I thought I could never find. I must be blessed because I found the miracle that I was looking for. All I had to do was look in her beautiful eyes.

She gave me a miracle, now it's up to me to help her find hers, and if it takes a million years to find it together, I will walk every step of the way. Not behind her, not ahead of her, but beside her every step of the way. If I make a promise in my lifetime, that's the promise I will keep until the end of time. Whatever she gives me, I will try to do the same and even more, but in reality, what she gave me was a perfect being. She is an angel, now I know I believe in angels because I see one every day. Heaven must be filled with angels like her. If she allows me to, I will live the rest of my life with her, trying to make her happy. Happiness takes a lifetime to achieve, and to achieve that, it has to be unconditional. She doesn't have to do anything for the rest of her life because I have found my miracle in her eyes. Now it will take a lifetime to repay her, but it's not like a debt that has to be repaid; rather, it's like a reason to live each lovely day that the Lord above has given to me to enjoy.

All our lives, we search for that pot of gold at the end of that rainbow, but some of us never find it. For me, I think I found the biggest pot of gold that ever could be allowed for one person to have in a lifetime. I finally experienced the power of love—I just hope that power never leaves because if it does, then life isn't worth living for. Deep down in my heart, it will never disappear because I will do everything in my power to preserve it to last an eternity.

No one can take that away from me because I have experienced life without that wonderful miracle, and now that I have it, I want to live the rest of my life as the complete person I now feel I am, all because I looked in her eyes.

I really cared about her, and I would do anything to go out with her. She always told me that she wasn't the type of woman for me. However, my stubbornness got in the way, and I took that as a challenge. The more times I saw her, the more I wanted to be with her. I used to time her on just about everything, like her breaks, lunchtime, etc. I really wanted to take her out, and I would do just about anything to fulfill my desire.

One time I saw her and noticed that she was very upset, but she wouldn't tell me why. Being the stubborn person that I am, I persisted, and she finally told me. Both of us had to go back to work, but I did finally get her telephone number, and that evening I called her. She was very surprised that I had called. We talked for a good hour on the phone, and she told me things that she wouldn't tell anyone else, including her family. That was another reason I liked her; she trusted me right away without any hesitation, so I had to be doing something right. She always told me that I was different from the rest of the men that she knew. That was a great compliment. By the same token, I thought to myself, 'What kind of men was she dating in the past?'

Over the next couple of weeks, we got very close, and we developed a stronger relationship. We went out for the first time on February 5, 1994. We went to this small restaurant in Bristol and enjoyed a perfect evening. By the end of the night, I was convinced that I wanted to spend the rest of my life with her. During that evening, I asked her to choose between three colors. Out of red, white, and yellow, what was her favorite? She answered "white" but wanted to know why. Thank God the waitress came around with our food, and I was able to avoid the question.

I called the florist and asked him to send a dozen long-stemmed white roses to her workplace on Valentine's Day. I went to work that Monday like it was a normal day, and five minutes after I sat down at my desk, she called me. She wanted to see me right away. I thought something was wrong, so I went to meet her. She came down to the seventh floor, and when the elevator opened up, she handed me a white stuffed monkey with a rose and wished me Happy Valentine's Day. I thanked her, kissed her, and went back to work. I was shocked, not because of the white monkey, but the fact that she remembered me on Valentine's Day. About 9:30 a.m., she called me to thank me for the beautiful white roses, now it was her turn to be shocked. All in all, it was a wonderful Monday because both of us were very happy.

From that point, I had fallen in love with her. She told me not to because I really didn't know that much about her. I told her I really didn't care about her past, and that what was in the past stays in the past. I knew she liked me very much, but I couldn't figure out the reason. I think it was because I was really nice to her, and she thought she was in a dream and that eventually I would change. I couldn't convince her that it just wasn't the case. When I like someone, I go the extra mile for them. I guess she had had bad relationships in the past, or maybe I was the opposite of anything she had experienced. Whatever the reason, I felt that deep down she really wanted to break things off because a dream doesn't last this long, and I guess she didn't want to get hurt. I knew she wasn't used to herself being the center of attention, and maybe it was my fault, but I gave her a lot of attention, and I guess it was more than she could handle.

One Friday night, we went to grab some dinner, and things were not as before...something was missing. I really believe that she wasn't used to a person like me, and she didn't know how to react to it. That Friday night was the last time I saw her. Of course, I was upset, but I thought with time that everything would be back to normal. I'm not sure why, but I always seem to recover. I think I have been hurt so many times that it has become second nature to me.

I always want to do the "right thing." At times, it doesn't work that way. Unfortunately, I try to analyze everything I do and every circumstance to the point that I always want to do the right thing. Then the frustration sets in. Because of my physical disability, I end up overcompensating in every situation. I came to realize that people sometimes take advantage of my gratefulness. I guess what I am trying to say is that I wear my heart on my sleeve, and some people will take advantage of my vulnerability. But that's the only way I know to survive. I thrive on people. I really will go the extra mile for anyone, but the thing is that I only see things in black and white, not shades of gray. It's not to say that I won't see gray (because if that were the case, I wouldn't be here today), but I really would like to know where a person is coming from. When I look into someone's eyes, I like to think that person is as genuine as I am, but most of the time it doesn't work that way, and I end up getting hurt. It's often my fault, because of my physical disability, I will pour out my heart to anyone who will listen, which leaves me very vulnerable. By wearing my heart on my sleeve, it is there to be crushed if you want to crush it. It's hard to change because I feel like I owe a lot to society. I tried to be the opposite way, but that didn't work either. I just have to be a little more selective, and someday I will not be so defenseless. In the meantime, it will all come out in the wash.

33

In May 1994, I was asked to be on the Board of Directors of United Cerebral Palsy of Rhode Island. I was thrilled and honored just to be considered by my peers. I thought it was great because it would give me a chance to be a positive role model for the handicapped community. I wanted to be more involved with the handicapped population, plus I brought tons of actual life experience to the board. I really had a tough schedule, but I enjoyed spending time with other people. I loved having people around me, and the more the better.

The rest of the members of the board voted me in. I went to my orientation on what was expected of board members. During that orientation, I learned that they wanted me to commit to being a VIP (Very Important Person). If I accepted the VIP challenge, I was responsible for bringing in $1500 to the agency. I accepted that challenge and thought that it was a simple task, especially for myself and the people I have known over the years. Plus, I always had a very vivid imagination and thought of a few events that would bring in the required monetary amount, so it didn't seem a burden to accept the challenge.

In the meantime, my brother Thomas's wife was expecting a child, and they called and said they wanted to speak to me.

I didn't have any idea what they wanted, but they came over to the house on a Sunday afternoon. They pulled me into the backyard. I thought I had done something wrong, and they were mad at me. My brother asked me if I would be their son's godfather. I was shocked and honored at the same time. I accepted, of course! After they left, I was still on cloud nine, but at the same time, I was a little terrified because I kind of felt like Thomas and Aida could have made a better choice, for two reasons. One, when you pick godparents, you usually have a married couple so that the child can know them as part of the family. I wasn't married at the time, and again, I was being selfish because I was thinking like an old-fashioned Portuguese man. People always told me that was the case before, but this was totally different. The second reason was that I still had cerebral palsy and still couldn't do some things physically like the average man. What would happen if my godchild wanted to take me ice skating? I would have to tell him that I couldn't do that. I spoke to the priest at my parish and told him about my feelings on the matter. He looked at me and said, "Why do you always beat yourself up, Joseph?" I said, "Father Greene, what do you mean?" He said, "Joseph, you are a wonderful man. Your brother picked you because you were their number one choice. We as humans tend to concentrate on the things we don't have. If only we concentrated on the gift God has given us, we would be fulfilled, both physically and spiritually." I thanked him and told him that he was right. What he had said made a lot of sense, and those words I kept in my heart and cherished.

One of the problems I have is that sometimes I don't give myself enough credit. It seems I am always apologizing for something that is not my fault. There are many things I have accomplished over the years, yet there is an ingredient missing. What that is, I don't know. All I know is I keep doing it without realizing that I am doing it. I tried to correct it over the years, and I am getting better at it. I think that maybe I feel like I have to apologize for my disability and the limitations that it causes me. I've been apologizing so long that it's become a habit that is tough to break. Another reason could be that, because of my cerebral palsy, I feel like I have to make the other person comfortable being with me, especially when I meet someone for the first time. They say first impressions are very important. I really want to make a big impression, so at the first meeting, I end up trying to cover up my disability. I really need to learn to accept my disability to the fullest because even though I have learned to deal with it, I need to accept it one hundred percent without any reservations, and become comfortable with myself.

God knows how hard I tried to really accept my disability, but still, I have days where I just can't. One day, my friend Roseanne's mother, Lucille Stringer, gave me a ride home right after the board meeting. I said, "Lucille, right at this moment in time, I have everything on course. Why then don't I have inner peace within myself?" She smiled and said, "Joseph, when you were born, how many handicapped people did you grow up with?" I said, "None." She said, "How many handicapped people did you know when you were growing up?" I said, "One, and that was William (Moose) Gordon." She said there is your answer. I looked at her, kind of puzzled and confused, and told her I didn't know what she was driving at. She said, "Joe, you are disabled, but you were not brought up in a disabled environment. You were brought up in a physically normal environment. Everything that you wanted in life, you had to fight, scratch, and claw to get it." I looked at her with tears in my eyes because I finally got the answer that I'd been looking for so many years. I felt like she had lifted a big, heavy burden off my shoulders. It wasn't a question of accepting my disability, because like she said, "Joe, you've already accepted your disability. If you hadn't, you wouldn't have accomplished the things you have accomplished over the years." I felt that was a turning point in my life. It also felt like my life had come full circle. I couldn't thank her enough.

Before my talk with Lucille, I believed that I would never accept my disability, because I always worked hard to maintain a high level of accomplishments, and my ego was also big enough to think I should reach that level. Instead of just accepting the way things were, I wanted to be the best I could be at that moment in time, or to go as far as I could beyond what my limitations should really let me do. When my limitations got in the way, that's when the frustrations started to accrue. As I mentioned before, I really had thought I had accepted my disability, but to really fully accept it without any reservations, I don't think I could ever accept it, because deep inside, I wanted more. In a way, that drove me to discover more talents that I didn't know I had. Sure, the frustration was always there; however, once I went beyond it, I learned. All in all, to sum up, most of my success in life came through trials and tribulations. Through that trial and error, stubbornness developed, and that was good because it made me a better and more positive person overall.

Through these trials and tribulations, I was writing more and more, but strangely enough, I began to really have an obsession to put everything on paper or computer, and then days or weeks later, I was amazed by what I had written. You know what is more amazing is the fact that I had a different perspective when it came to different conclusions, not a right or wrong answer, but a different view about things. For example, once when I was still living in California, I went to breakfast, sat down at the counter, and noticed a lady who kept staring at me. She wanted to ask what was wrong with me, but she was afraid to ask. So, I introduced myself, with my speech impediment, and I explained cerebral palsy to her. I gave her a lot of credit because most strangers that I have met over the years were afraid to ask what cerebral palsy is. But she wasn't afraid to ask, and she did.

After explaining to her what cerebral palsy was and what caused it, she had more questions about the disability. The only thing I could think of was a broken arm or leg. She told me that she had broken her arm while skiing, and I thought it was the perfect example to use. I asked her how long she had been in the cast, and she said about eleven weeks. I asked her if she had constantly thought of the broken arm. She said that she hadn't, except when she couldn't do certain things. I asked her how she handled that, and she said she had to find a different way to accomplish what she wanted to do. She had really answered her own question. I told her that I don't think about cerebral palsy twenty-four hours a day, but only when I can't do something because my CP gets in the way. Then I have to find another solution. I think one of the best ways to explain how CP affects me to people who are not disabled is to use that analogy.

I think everybody who has ever lived must have a personal ultimate battle, like my story that I shared earlier. This is my own daily personal battle. But I really believe that these personal battles are good for the person who goes through them because they really build character and personal strength. I can always tell a strong person just by their own personal battle. The way a person handles their personal battle really shows what they are made of. The person who conquers these battles often wins trials and tribulations that life presents to them. Success begins with these personal battles, and I don't think there is a person who is successful who hasn't gone through them.

Through life's problems come personal gains and satisfactions that often come through living through the eyes of other people and personalities. I really think that each person you have met and will meet will have a direct impact on your life, whether positive or negative. It is really up to you whether you accept or reject a certain situation. If you think of a situation in your life and the choices you made during that situation, consider what would have happened if you had gone the other way. Where would you be? It is up to you to change to a positive perspective so that it can benefit you. Maybe not today, but in the days, months, and years to come it will have a direct effect on your thinking.

34

September rolled along, and Victoria's birthday was on the 28th of the month. We hadn't been in contact for a few months, and I really didn't know how she would react if I sent her a birthday card. I contemplated whether to send her one or not. You see, she had a special place in my life even though we had only known each other for a year or so. I felt that I had known her all my life. When I looked at her for the first time, walking with that cane, it automatically developed a special bond between us that would never be broken, no matter what. I decided to send her a card and hope for the best. When she received the card, she was surprised because I remembered her birthday, and she called me at work to thank me. I got to thinking that even though we hadn't seen each other for a few months, she still had kept my telephone number, so that meant that she was thinking of me also. Be that as it may, I was just hoping that she and I could pick up that friendship that was pretty strong in the past. We were both stubborn in our beliefs, but that is what made her stand apart from the rest of the other women I have met over the years. There was a special aura about her. I will give you a quick example. I took a lady out to dinner, and her name was Veronica. We sat down and started to talk, and I looked her right in the eye and called her Victoria. She said, "What did you say?" and I said, "Victoria." Well, it's not right to call someone by someone else's name, and she got up and walked out on me at dinner. I was upset, not because she walked out on me, but because I couldn't take the name Victoria out of my mind. There was something that special about her.

Whether or not things would be better in the future remained to be seen. As you probably know by now, I am not, and I repeat, I am not a patient person. I always believe that if there is something within your control that you can change, then you should do it. I still had a long way to go. By the same token, because of my lack of patience and my strong stubbornness, I was a person with a hunger for a better tomorrow. Now that sounds strange because it goes over and above any rule that our parents taught us over the years. My parents taught me the basics about life, but still, I always wanted to do it my way, whether or not it was good for me. For the most part, I truly believe that it has helped me over the years. Could it be that I had something to prove to myself or my community? Whatever the case, I just wanted the chance to add my two cents in. At this time, I began to see my cerebral palsy as a blessing in my life because my will wouldn't die. I had an advantage over the average person in society because I was normal, but I was also disabled. To me, that was a tremendous advantage.

On September 17, 1994, Tommy's wife gave birth to a healthy baby boy. They named the child Jacob Joseph Ferreira. That was a great honor for me; this was the second time one of my brothers had named a child for me. I felt that was a great tribute because it showed the deep love that my brothers have for me. September 17 is also an important date because it is our youngest brother Victor's birthday as well. I guess I can't forget their birthdays now! I was really excited because

I knew I was going to be a godfather, and to me, that was the next best thing to being a father—something that I often prayed for but knew I needed to wait for God to give me that opportunity. I just needed to be patient because my life had been based on miracle after miracle, and I knew that this was a miracle that was going to take place someday. Jacob filled some of that void for the time being, and he was a beautiful baby. I was honored and privileged to be his godfather. I kept thinking, maybe one day, that I will meet my future wife and she will give me the biggest miracle of all—a child of my own.

That was the only thing that was out of my control—having a child. Not for nothing, but before I died, I wanted to have a child or children. Because I was limited physically, I just wanted to have a physically normal child who would call me Daddy. Maybe I was being selfish, but to see my wonderful nephews growing up before my eyes and knowing that I didn't have one of my own made it really tough, especially during the holidays. Christmas is a very special time of the year. In my way of thinking, Christmas is for children, especially when they open up a present—a million dollars could never buy that beautiful moment that children give us grown-ups. We should learn a lot from children, especially during Christmas time. Certainly, money can go a long way, but it's not important on that wonderful day we call Christmas. I was still hoping and praying to meet that wonderful woman to bring that wonderful child into my life. God is the greatest matchmaker, and I knew that He had a special lady waiting for me. There was no doubt in my mind that I would meet her at some point in my life, but at that time, it was really tough. I just had to hope and pray that I would meet her soon, because it really was hard to be the only one in the family without a child. My brothers downplayed it a lot, saying that marriage wasn't all it was cracked up to be, and that it takes a lot of practice to make a relationship work. They were right, and I knew it was an everyday, ongoing process. But if you were to meet a good couple who were happily married and ask them if they had a chance to do it all over again, would they make the same choice? Their reply would be yes within a heartbeat or less. It's very hard to find that special person, but when you find them, you will do everything in your power to preserve the relationship no matter what the circumstances.

I just believe that a good man will always have a good lady by his side. And a good lady will always have a good man by her side. In a good relationship, neither one walks ahead of or behind the other; instead, they walk side by side. When two people get married, it is like dying of self and giving of self to the other person. I found that in my brothers' marriages, and I wanted it for myself, but unless I found that same love that they had, then I would wait for the right person. I decided I wouldn't compromise. My compromising days were over; I had learned that life is hard, and I wasn't about to go through a bad relationship just for the sake of getting married. Until I found that perfect relationship that was defined by the word "perfect," I wasn't going to compromise, especially since I knew that she was out there lurking. One day our eyes will meet, and until then I will just have to wait for her.

All in all, I had everything that a man could possibly want. I wasn't completely satisfied, but I was content with the things I had accomplished and the way things were going. For the most part, they were going pretty well. I always wanted to do more. I think that was my nature. I really started to reflect on the things that mattered the most, such as my family, friends, the person that I was, and the intangible assets that I had. Up to that point, it was an ongoing process to get where I was, with a lot of struggles, but that was the challenge before me, and I never turned down a challenge.

Part Four

35

Challenges are won and lost within oneself. I really believe that. However, if you have the attitude that you have a slim glimmer of hope, I bet that you will overcome the biggest obstacle that stands before you. Most battles that we encounter are mentally challenging. *By the same token, you should never set a timetable because no matter what challenge it is, if you set a timetable, then you have defeated the purpose. For all intents and purposes, the challenge before you will have defeated you.*

My personal challenges have taken years to conquer. Now, have I conquered all of them? No, of course not, but I have conquered many and I am proud of these accomplishments.

One of my biggest concerns is that when my mind tells me that I can overcome every challenge that stands before me, it can be scary. I get comfortable thinking that I can do anything. That is a sure sign of stupidity, and most of all a sign of arrogance, because there are things that I am not meant to do. When you think you have it all, then there will be a day when everything will come crashing down on you, and you won't be able to come out of it. Everyday challenges are hard enough, and if we are thinking about tomorrow's challenges and we haven't met today's challenges, then we are headed on a downward spiral. We don't want to do that, we want to be on a steady upswing, and it doesn't matter how long it takes as long as we go up. The important thing for every passing day is that we progress and not digress. Today's challenges are hard enough just to get through the day. We cannot look back on yesterday's challenges except to learn from them, because we can't change the way we met those challenges.

We had our annual Christmas party coming up with UCP. There was only one lady that I had in mind to ask, and that was Victoria. I called her and asked her if she would like to go with me, and she said yes. I was happy and excited because she was one lady who always added spark to my life. Like I mentioned before, a good man always has a good lady by his side, and for some unknown reason, she always brought out the best in me. I always thought that she looked wonderful in red, so I asked her if she would wear something red, and she agreed. Unfortunately, the Christmas party was during the middle of the week, and Victoria and I had to work the next day. I spoke with my supervisor, and he let me leave early from work. Victoria wanted to pick me up, but I told her that was crazy because she would be going in the opposite direction of the party. I arranged for Victor to drive me to her house, and then she could drive to the party. My brothers were always wonderful because whatever I lacked, Michael, Thomas, or Victor would fill the void. That night, Victor was available to drive me.

When he dropped me off, Victoria came outside to meet me, and she looked simply beautiful. Victor asked if I needed a ride home, and she said that she would take me home. I couldn't take my eyes off of her.

Red was her color, and not seeing her for the last few months was truly worth the wait. We arrived at the party and started to introduce ourselves to the other guests. Some of the board members were also there. We went to get a drink, and Victoria and I started to reminisce about the fun we had in the past. She also told me that I acted like a nut; however, it was a good nut. I couldn't take my eyes off of her. She was the best-looking woman there, and that's saying something because there were quite a few ladies there.

The president of the board, David Monte, and his wife wanted to buy Victoria and me a drink. I insisted that I would buy all of us a drink, and this went back and forth for a couple of minutes. Finally, Victoria tapped me on the knee under the table, and I stopped and let David buy the drink. I excused myself from the table, but she excused herself as well and followed me to the lobby. She looked at me and said I was stubborn. I didn't understand and asked her why she thought I was stubborn. She said that it was because David wanted to buy us a drink, and I had insisted on paying. I told her I enjoyed paying. She said she understood that, but that other people also get pleasure from buying me something, and I always refused.

You know, she was right. I think that over the years, because of my CP, I felt like I had to overcompensate for my disability, and that shouldn't have been the case. Victoria taught me a very valuable lesson: that because of my stubbornness, I was essentially stopping people from doing good deeds. Stubbornness is good, but if it's going to hinder people from doing acts of kindness, they end up being hurt. She also told me that she didn't go out with me because of my CP, but rather because of the type of person that I was. I really thought that I had everything together, but after she told me this, I guess I needed to reconsider.

That night, I had to make a promise to her to be a little less stubborn and let people around me do what they wanted to do without saying no. I agreed, because she was right. She also threatened me by saying, with her beautiful smile, that if I didn't become a little less stubborn, she wouldn't see me anymore. How could I do anything but agree when she looked at me with those miracle eyes? The rest of the night was great. Somehow, I also felt like a great burden had been lifted off my shoulders, finally realizing that by being stubborn, I could limit other people. People had been telling me this over the years, but it was Victoria who really helped me understand what they had been trying to say.

We left the party because both of us had work the next morning. On the way home, we started talking about my stubbornness and the fact that I didn't have to be stubborn. She also told me that my stubbornness drove people away. I couldn't even debate with her because I knew she was right. I knew it was something I really needed to work on. She also told me that I should learn to take more instead of always giving. I told her that I felt like that over the years, I had taken enough, and that I needed to give back more. She asked me, "Why do you always feel that you owe society? I am sure that whatever society gave you, you have repaid a hundredfold, so please learn to take a little more!" I smiled and thanked her because if we hadn't talked about it that night, I would never have realized this, and it would have taken years to see what I was doing to myself. She was right, but I still didn't want to give up on other people because people hadn't given up on me. If I see people who are trying but need a little help, I like to be able to help them.

36

I learned at a very early age in my life that people are very important. I also learned that if you admire a person, then you should become a sponge and absorb everything about that person. Then you are ahead of the game and a better person for it. You know, I've been astonished that people have come up to me and said that I was amazing and thanked me for my advice. I began to wonder if this was all due to my disability, or would people regard me the same way if I was not disabled? I think the answer would be no, because through my disability, I have learned about special needs that others may have. I would say that my disability gave me a special insight at a much earlier age than I ordinarily would have had. I think disabled people develop a sixth sense. I can't explain it, but I think I was given a special gift in place of what had been taken away from me. Whatever the reason, I am glad I have it and I am not complaining, because I have been able to help people with it.

The person who did accounts payable, Harold Gould, retired. He was a sweet elderly gentleman whom I loved and respected very much. I was sad that he was retiring because whenever I had a question, he was there to give me the right answer or the best advice that a seventy-six-year-old man could give me. He was my reinforcement; whenever things didn't go right, he was there to see me through. On the other hand, I was glad he was going to be able to enjoy his retirement because he worked hard over the years, and he deserved it.

I knew his job entailed much more than I was used to and that my responsibilities would increase more and more each day. Deep down in my heart, I believed that I was up to the task, and I trusted in my abilities and capabilities. It was only a matter of time, so I thought that I would be poised and relaxed to do a good job, one that I thought I could and should do well.

When Hall retired, I was really scared because from then on, I would be on my own. Whatever I did, I would reap the rewards or pay the consequences. The first couple of months, I thought I did a good job, but there was an uneasy feeling in the pit of my stomach. All my life, I was under the gun, but I always met the challenges and overcame my fears. All I had to do was stay focused, and everything would fall into place. However, I would miss him because he was a true gentleman in every respect of the word. He was a true mentor.

Victoria and I weren't really working out as far as a boyfriend/girlfriend relationship. I guess the harder I tried, the worse it got. Finally, I came to the realization that friendship was as close as we would ever get. It was hard to accept, but when you try your best and it doesn't work out, then you have to let it go. Finally, I said enough is enough, and I learned to accept that. Even though I didn't like it, I had to face the fact that a friendship would be the best relationship Victoria and I would accomplish.

I was alone again, but I had things to keep my mind occupied. Fate can take a strange twist in life without you realizing what is going on. Where I was working, I would meet a lot of different people every day, including a man named Jesse Crum. One day, he asked me why I didn't have a relationship. I told him that I had found that it was hard to meet the right person. I wanted to find a special lady because I had had my fill of disappointment. He looked at me and said, "If I introduce you to someone, would you be interested in going out to dinner with me and my wife?" I said sure, but I wasn't going to count on it. If it happened, it happened, but I wasn't going to lose sleep over it.

I was going through my everyday routine for about two weeks when the phone rang. It was Jesse, and he said he had found a lady he wanted me to meet and wanted us all to go out to dinner. I accepted, and we made plans to go the upcoming Saturday. I asked him for more details, but all he gave me was that her name was Susan, that she was a lady, and that was the end of the conversation. We met in the lobby at work several times over the next week, but Jesse wouldn't give me any more details; all he said was to wait until Saturday...so I had to wait until Saturday. Unfortunately, it snowed, and the date got canceled. I thought it was strange because up until then, we had had a mild winter with no major snowstorms to talk about. I told myself I had to have been born under a black cloud because when something looked good, it usually fell apart or didn't happen. If it wasn't for bad luck, I would have no luck at all!

I went to work the following Monday, and when I saw Jesse, I tried to reschedule the date. I told Jesse maybe it would be better if we got together when I got back from Florida. (I was planning a vacation with Gary, my best friend.) But Jesse insisted that we should go out this Saturday, so I agreed. The following Saturday, Victor gave me a ride to Jesse's house, and we waited for Susan. Finally, Susan got there, and we were introduced. She seemed pleasant enough. We had time to talk while Jesse and his wife Donna finished getting ready.

Jesse drove, and we went to pick up another couple who were going to join us. Jesse asked where there was a good place to eat in Bristol. I suggested a good restaurant, and Jesse had heard about it from a friend, but when we got there, the restaurant was going up in smoke from a grease fire that started in the kitchen. Just my luck, right? We moved on to another restaurant that was still intact, with no smoke coming out of the kitchen! It was a fine evening, but one thing that stood out was that Donna kept asking Susan what I was saying. My speech impediment really interferes with people being able to understand me, and I'm hard to understand at first. Susan understood every word I was saying, which really impressed me. I came to find out that Susan had a nephew with cerebral palsy. She explained that to me, and all through dinner, I kept seeing those intangible things that we look for in people.

After dinner, we agreed to go dancing. Now I hadn't been dancing in years, but I thought it would be fun. We all got in the van, and I noticed Jesse was taking wide turns around the corners. Every time he did this, I would end up in Susan's lap! It was funny because we both knew what Jesse was up to, and we laughed. We had a really good conversation. I liked her because she came from a good family background, with good morals and values, something that was hard to come by.

This blind date really turned out to be a diamond in the rough. I was really very interested in her. I was having a great time, and I really couldn't remember a time like this. If there was one, it was quite some time in the past. Whatever the reason, I was glad I met her.

Finally, we got to the club, and we sat down and ordered some drinks. When the music started, Jesse and Donna hit the dance floor, as did the other couple, Ray and Pat. This left

Susan and me alone to talk. Jesse insisted that we two were to join them on the dance floor. I looked at Susan and asked her to dance, and she agreed. It felt nice because I felt that Susan wanted to be there, and she seemed to really enjoy my company. The feeling was definitely mutual.

It was getting late, and like everything else that's good, the night had to come to an end. On the way home, we started to kiss, and Jesse was watching, so his right and left turns got wider and wider. Instead of me falling on Susan, she was falling on me! I asked Susan if she wanted to go out again, and she said yes. I asked her for her phone number, and she gave it to me. I finally got home at 2:30 in the morning. I just couldn't remember when I had so much fun. The time had simply flown. I got to my room and started to recap the night. There were so many good memories in one night that I couldn't count them all. If I had tried, I wouldn't have been able to get to sleep. Deep down, I knew I had met someone really special.

In the morning, I called Susan to thank her for the wonderful night. She thanked me as well. I also told her that I hadn't had a night like that in such a long time. I was really glad to have met her, and I also wanted to see her again. She asked, "What about next Friday?" I told her, "Yes!!"

I don't really know why, but it seemed like I had known her for a while, but I didn't want to get caught up in that feeling because whenever I did that, I ended up heading for a big disappointment. I tried very hard to not think about it, but it was no use. That Sunday, I went to church as usual, and I thanked God for the wonderful time I had had. I sort of challenged Him and told Him if this was from His doing, to please let it continue, but if I was going to get hurt, please let us know before we got any deeper.

She had been hurt before, too. She was married once

before, but it didn't last. And I had been hurt numerous times, and I was tired of dead ends. I liked her, and she liked me, so I didn't want things to go wrong. But you know, once I said that prayer, I got a warm feeling inside that made me feel very assured that I was doing something right. It was a wonderful feeling.

The following day, I went to work with a terrific attitude. People actually asked me if I was all right, and I couldn't help but tell them everything was wonderful. I had people come to me and say, "Joe, you are always a nice guy, but today you seem like you've found something you were looking for." I said, "Yes, what I was long searching for, I believe I have found. I just didn't want to lose this feeling."

Susan called me at work that day, and it was really nice to hear her voice. Actually, it was a pleasant surprise because it had been a tough day, but for some reason, after I heard her voice, everything fell into place. She just wanted to see how I was doing. Hearing from her put everything in perspective. After the phone call, the roof could have fallen in, and I wouldn't have cared.

I had some time to myself, and I went to get a cup of coffee. I started thinking (sometimes that's dangerous!) that, especially for someone like myself, it was amazing how one person and one moment could change one's whole outlook in life. It was simply a feeling that I couldn't describe. I mean, in your heart, you know what you want to say, but when it comes out, you just can't find the right words. The rest of the day was just perfect.

It was amazing because one of us always called the other just at the right moment. People at work commented on my new energy, especially in the afternoon. I just told them it was a new vitamin I was trying out. I didn't want to get my hopes up, plus I was sick and tired of false hopes and empty promises. I just wanted to be sure that this relationship was going in the right direction. I know one thing though...I was very happy, and when I was with her, nothing else seemed to matter.

The following Friday, we discussed going to see her friend Norman in Cumberland. Victor picked me up and took me to Susan's place of work. After she got done, she took me to her house. I was still amazed at the way her parents seemed to have taken to me so easily.

I was taken aback because I was disabled, and they were able to look beyond that. The other thing that was astonishing to me was that Susan had been married before, and I would have thought that her parents would have been skeptical about another man being in Susan's life, but that wasn't the case. Susan went downstairs to change, and I stayed upstairs talking to her parents. After she came back, I said good night, and her mom kissed me. Susan was shocked because her mother had never done that before, not even to Susan's ex-husband, never mind the fact that this was the first time we had met. That really made me feel pretty good.

We got to Norman's house, and he was very pleasant and made me feel right at home. Norman is a pretty straightforward kind of guy. He looked at me and said, "Joe, you seem like a pretty nice guy, and Susan likes you, but if you hurt her, you are going to deal with me." I looked at him and said, "Understood, but what happens if she hurts me?" He was stunned because he didn't know what to say. I guess he was waiting for me to give him a smart answer, but I didn't. He looked at Susan and said, "You know, Sue, I like him because I would never expect him to answer a question with a question." It was a great evening, and everything went well. Even though Norman was strong, he was honest and sincere, and showed his concern for Susan, which I liked.

We left his house and headed to my house. Of course, I didn't drive, so Susan drove me home. From Norman's house in Cumberland to my house in Bristol, it takes one hour and fifteen minutes, but Susan didn't seem to mind. I was bothered because after dropping me off, she had to drive to her house, which took another half hour. Here I am home, and she was driving home alone. All I did was to pace back and forth until she got home. I didn't get ready for bed until I knew for sure she was safe and sound.

My company was offering cellular phones, and I really thought it would be a good idea to get one for Susan. Then and only then would I really have peace of mind. We got the phone at a fraction of the retail cost. Susan wanted to give me the number, but I was worried about getting in the habit of calling her too often, because in those days it was very costly. I finally got the number, and my parents had it too. We were the only people who had it. It was funny because the first couple of days, someone called it looking for "Tom" (not my brother). I jokingly told her she was passing out the number already. We had to get a credit from the phone company.

I was very happy with the way things were going, but I kept waiting for the proverbial other shoe to drop. Someone told me, "Joe, don't question it, just accept it. You've been a good person; now it's your turn to be happy. All your life you have given and given, now learn to take a little." I knew she was right, but still, I felt I hadn't done anything to be this happy. In reality, I was punishing myself, but from that time on, I tried to learn to accept the good things that were happening to me. It seemed strange, but it felt good. It also seemed that Susan gave me newfound energy. After a good talk with my friend Marcia, everything seemed to get into perspective. Of course, my family had been telling me this for years, but do you think I would listen? It always takes another person outside the family in order to make it sink in.

One thing I forgot to mention: When Gary and I got back from Florida, guess who was waiting for me at the airport? You guessed it—Susan! I mention this now because back then, I was developing feelings for Susan, but I really didn't want to show them because I had been hurt enough times over the years that I was still being cautious, and I didn't want to go through that again. I was stunned when I saw her at the airport, but right then it was confirmed in my heart that this lady was something special. Things kept rolling right along, and for the first time in a long time, I was enjoying myself.

37

I started to reflect on my life and the things I had accomplished, and was pretty happy the way things turned out. I was also very pleased that good things, to my amazement, were happening to me. Even though there were a lot of frustrations and bitterness, I realized I wouldn't have had it any other way. I realized I was happy with the way things had turned out. I still felt I had a lot to accomplish, but now I had finally met someone whom I could put my whole trust into without getting hurt. Susan was a blessing in disguise, even though she may disagree with that statement. I know differently, and she won't change my mind. She really has been a wonderful BLESSING in my life. Still, she would argue the point and tell you that I am the one who changed her life.

It's funny having cerebral palsy. It really disappeared when I met her. My wonderful mother used to cater to me. That would burn Susan up because she knew I could do a lot of things if I put my mind to them, but my mother had done everything for me. I really didn't use my right hand too much until I met Susan. Now I do plenty more with it. One time, I remember asking Susan for a glass of soda, and she refused, saying, "Go get it yourself." She told me to do it, so I did and spilled it all over the floor. I got upset because she hadn't done it for me. She said, "Now I know you can't carry liquid, but at least you tried." She continued, "Joseph, I would do anything for you, but first you have to try," and we both agreed to that. Susan helped me find abilities that I really thought I didn't have. For the first time in a long time, I really found someone who cared for me as a person and accepted me for who I was.

We really didn't see too much of each other because our jobs didn't really allow it, plus she lived in Cranston, which was about thirty minutes from Bristol. We talked over the telephone a lot, and spent the weekends together. One Saturday night, her mother asked me to stay over at the house instead of having Susan drive me back to Bristol and then drive herself home. Susan's mouth dropped because her mother had never asked a man to stay overnight. Of course, I stayed on the couch, but for her mother to say that meant I must have been doing something right. Her father seemed to like me as well and was always giving me good advice. The next morning, we got up and went to church, and then grabbed lunch.

I was very happy with the way things were working out. My parents liked her, my brothers liked her, my nephews adored her, and my friends liked her. My best friend thought she was the best thing that ever happened to me, and he was right. My sisters-in-law liked her too, especially Maria, because both she and Susan were hairdressers, which gave them a bond. Maria was my hairdresser, but she convinced Susan to cut my hair. It gave Maria a break because whenever she cut my hair, I was like a little boy; I never sat still in the chair. I think from that day on, Susan gave me my new nickname, which was "rascal." Susan finally gave in and agreed to cut my hair. She didn't really want to do it because I was Maria's client, and because she really didn't like to cut anyone's throat, but Maria gave her blessing.

Susan and I were discussing where we would live after we

were married. I wanted to live in Bristol, where I grew up. Susan had a different perspective and said, "Your parents have four sons, and my parents only have me who can help them. They are getting on in years, and they rely on me quite a bit." Susan was right, and who was I to take their daughter away from them? We decided to look at condominiums. We thought they would be the best solution, because they would be easier to keep up, especially in the winter. We started looking around and we found a few we liked. Still, Susan was concerned that her annulment hadn't come in yet. I looked at her and said, "I am going to marry you and not the church. Now it would be nice to have a church wedding, but it's not the end of the world. It will arrive in its own time; you are not going to change anything, so just stop worrying." Susan was concerned about my father, who wanted me to have a church wedding. I told her again that a church wedding would be nice, but God knows our hearts, and He is watching us.

Susan got busy with the invitations, gathering family and friends. It was a nice time, but a nervous time. I questioned my ability to be the head of a household. Growing up in a Portuguese family, my father was the head of our house. Even with my doubts about being disabled, I try to maintain a confident outlook on life. I just have to take it one step at a time and keep moving forward. If I fall, there's always someone to pick me up, dust me off, and put me back in the right direction.

Susan asked Donna to be her maid of honor. I was torn between Jesse, Donna's husband, my best friend, Gary, and one of my brothers as my best man. I ended up choosing Jesse; not only was he the person who introduced me to Susan, but he was also Donna's husband. The time was closer to the wedding, and still no word on the annulment. I contacted one of the attorneys at work to see if he knew a Justice of the Peace, and he found me one. Of course, my father wasn't crazy about the idea, but my mother talked sense into him. I basically told him that if we don't get married by the Justice of the Peace, then we might as well live together unmarried. He finally gave us his blessing, and to be honest, that was more important to me especially because I was his firstborn.

After a couple of weeks searching for a condominium, we found one that we liked. Edwards and Angel gave me an attorney, Robert Arena, for the closing, and the firm didn't charge for his time. Susan put down a $1400 deposit, and we closed on the condominium on September 17, 1996. The wedding was to be held on November 16, 1996, so it was an exciting year. All the preparations were nearly complete, and things were moving right along. The days were going by fast. I kept saying my life with Susan was real! Even if it did feel as good as a dream. She was a wonderful lady to boot, someone that I could trust and share my dreams with. It was reality, and I had found a partner to spend the rest of what God brought to me. It was like a fairy tale, only it was reality and something that was going to flourish into something beautiful and special. All those years of being a third wheel were about to change now that I had Susan by my side, someone who could understand me and my struggles in life. I had waited a long time for this. In a couple of months, two people would be ready to commit to a partnership —a partnership that had taken a long time to form, but like anything else, was something that would be cherished because it had been worth waiting for.

My mother was very happy for me. She and I always had good conversations; she was my rock and my wonderful, sweet lady. She always took a backseat to everyone. She was a very humble lady who always made people feel special. No matter what the circumstances, she made you feel special. One day, I came home after work, and she was smiling, and I asked her why she was smiling. She looked at me, kissed me, and said,

"I told you that if you were patient enough, everything would fall into place." She was right; she always told me to wait, and something good would change for the better. That conversation that we had showed me that everything good in life does take time, and if it's worth it, then you keep it in your heart until it comes to pass. That lady has so much wisdom and knowledge, and I can say every conversation with her was a learning experience. I was truly blessed to have her as a mother and a friend.

My brothers took our father and me out to dinner, since my last few days of being a bachelor were fast approaching. We had a great time. We talked about our relationship, and I thanked all of them because growing up, my brothers were my shield. I told them that without them, I wouldn't be the person that I am because they always treated me as their equal, and they respected me as a person. They insisted that I gave them strength because they had seen my everyday struggles, but I was the one who gained strength from them. It was a really great dinner. Even my father was proud of me. Although he never said it, I could see in his eyes. It was a fun-filled evening with my brothers and my father.

When you pick up your tuxedo, you know the time is near to get married. All that week, the butterflies stayed in my stomach; in fact, here's how nervous I was: my dad had to shave me all week, not one day but all week. "I've wanted this day all my life, so why am I getting nervous?" I asked myself. It was a new beginning with Susan. This was all I ever wanted. I guess facing the unknown will always rattle anyone. Susan didn't want any bridesmaids, just a Maid of Honor. Jesse was my best man, and Michael, Thomas, Victor, and Gary were my ushers. After thirty-eight years, I was finally getting married, a great feeling, but still with butterflies in my stomach. I assured my dad that once the annulment came in, I would get married by the church. He looked at me and said, "Just be happy." I replied, "I am." Finally, November 17th came, the day that two hearts would become one, two people starting a new adventure and a journey of marriage. The guests were seated at their table, and everything was in place to say our vows. We stood together in front of the Justice of the Peace.

Susan looked beautiful. I was repeating what I was told to repeat, and I was shaking in my shoes. I couldn't put the ring on Susan's finger—that's how nervous I was! Then she repeated her vows to me, and those words were special, not only to hear them, but because those words were meant toward me. Then the Justice of the Peace introduced us as husband and wife, and all the nervousness went away that very second. We had ninety-eight guests at the wedding, mostly from my side, because Susan said to me, "Joseph, I have been married and I want this day to be special for you," and it was. It was one of the best days of my life. Everyone seemed to have enjoyed themselves. What a great time! Susan and I didn't go anywhere for our honeymoon. We thought that buying the condominium was far more important at the time. The next morning, we opened our eyes and I said, "Good morning, Mrs. Ferreira, how does it feel to be called that?" and she said, "It feels wonderful!" I vowed to myself that even though she married someone disabled, she wouldn't lack anything, a vow that I will hold until I die.

38

One thing happened during this time that made us sad. November 20th was my mother's birthday, and we found out that my grandmother, my father's mother, who still lived in Portugal, had passed away on my mother's birthday. It was a bittersweet day, but it could not change how happy we were. We wanted to start a family right away, given our ages.

Day after day and month after month, we could not conceive a child. Susan went through all kinds of tests and medications, and still was barren. I joined a bible study, and I even had the bible study group praying for us. In the meantime, the annulment came in, and we could get our marriage blessed by the church. We decided to ask Gary and his wife to stand up for us at the ceremony. They accepted the invitation, and we talked to the priest of the church. We wanted September 14th because that was my in-laws' wedding anniversary. In a way, that was a good day, because that way I would never forget our anniversary, because my father-in-law would remind me!

We usually went to church services at 12:00 noon. After the service, everyone left except the whole family, along with Gary and Pat. The priest gave us a nice ceremony and blessed our marriage according to the Catholic faith, and then all of us went out to lunch. We invited the priest, but he had a previous obligation. Susan was getting frustrated about getting pregnant and even asked me to get tested. I really didn't want to, but I wanted to be a father in the worst way, so I told Susan right after we said our vows at church that I would make the appointment to get tested. My father was happy that we got our marriage blessed, and quite frankly, I was too. After a time, Susan said to me, "Joseph, it doesn't seem I am going to get pregnant, so I am going off the medication, because it is playing havoc with my body and making me have mood swings. I supported her all the way, but I did tell her that I was going to get tested, and then after that, whatever happened would happen. She started to cry and said that people always get pregnant, and they abort their babies, and others who want babies can't have them—it wasn't fair. I said that she was a woman of faith, and whatever happened to her, not to lose that faith. She said, "I won't, but it's very discouraging not to have a child when it's made out of love." I smiled and told her, "Whatever happens, it will be for the best, just keep your trust in God because nothing else matters."

She happened to have an appointment with her doctor the following Monday. She asked if I would get upset if she told the doctor no more medication, and I said, Of course not. I went to work that following Monday morning, and Susan had the doctor's appointment. I got a phone call from her at 11:20 in the morning. I thought she was going to remind me to call the doctor to schedule an appointment so I could get tested, when I knew I had already told her I was going to call on my lunch hour. She told me that wasn't the reason she was calling me, and then I became concerned. Then she said that the reason she was calling was to tell me that she was pregnant. I was so excited that I couldn't contain myself! I started to cry. My supervisor came over to find out what was wrong. I told him what happened, and he was very excited for me. A few weeks later, she went back to the doctor for a checkup, and she found out that the baby was a girl. At first, I was hesitant to find out. Susan gave me the option of knowing or not. I did not want to know, but I didn't always like surprises, so I told her to tell me. I was very happy to know that it was a girl! I really thought that it would be a boy, because my mother and father had four boys and their sons had all boys, so I just thought I would have a boy, but it was a girl in the womb. Everyone was happy for me because they all knew how much I wanted a child and how much I wanted to be a father. My mother said with her humor, "You finally did right, and I finally got the girl that I always wanted!" You see, my mom always wanted a girl, and when we came to America, she conceived another child. It was a baby girl, but her daughter was stillborn and so never made it. My mother said, "My family is complete with you giving me the baby that I always wanted," and she hugged and kissed me. She also said to me, "A long time ago, Joe, you might have looked like the weak link of the family, but with that link you showed that you were the stronger one. There's a reason why you were born disabled, and that reason was to make everyone who comes in contact with you better. I am so proud to be your mother."

My mom is a very wise lady, not educated, but always speaking from the heart. The heart always speaks the truth and never lies. At the same time, we found out that my Uncle Antonio had cancer. Antonio was everyone's favorite uncle. My wife and I visited him at the hospital, and I told him that he needed to get better because Susan was pregnant, and he had to see his great-niece. He smiled and said, "I will do my best." That evening we went to bed. We usually talked before going to sleep. I was rubbing her stomach gently, and I said to her, "Getting married by the Justice of the Peace was nice, but as soon as we got our marriage blessed, you got pregnant."

Susan called it fate because we both wanted a child. Of course, my theory made more sense, and I still believe that God had blessed us when we got our marriage blessed. Regardless, I was going to be a daddy, and it was a great feeling.

On October 19th, 1997, my uncle Antonio passed away, a wonderful man whom everyone loved. He had a wife and four boys. I was hoping that he would be alive when our daughter was born because she would have loved him like everyone has over the years. He was truly a special person and a special uncle. When I found that Susan was pregnant, I started the countdown for when our daughter was going to be born. My coworkers would come to me and ask me, "Why are you so relaxed?" Just knowing that I was going to be a dad was a great feeling.

39

Susan's doctor gave us a due date, so I took out my desk calendar and made a countdown for when my daughter was supposed to be born. I don't think there was a more exciting time than knowing that I was going to be a father. I had seen all my nephews being born and my brothers being excited, and now I had the same feeling that they did, and it was a great feeling. I came home from work one evening, and Susan and I were having supper, and I chuckled. She asked me, "What's so funny?" I looked at her and said, "You know we got married by the Justice of the Peace? We started trying to have a family, you went through a lot of tests and medications that your doctor recommended, and nothing happened. Only when we got our marriage blessed did you get pregnant. I think that's amazing because I live by faith." Susan looked at me and said, "Funny, but I remember when I got pregnant, I just knew I was going to get pregnant that night." Faith can play a major role in someone's life. Faith can get you through a stage in life when all you have is faith. I do believe that faith was the primary factor in my wife getting pregnant. What was also interesting was that my wife had stopped all medication that her doctor prescribed for her, and she relied on her faith. Faith is a powerful aid in helping us believe in our abilities and ourselves. No one can give it to you; it comes from your inner being.

Always believe in yourself because it will help you reach your potential. Always set goals for yourself and stay focused on those goals. The only thing that can stop those goals from happening is you, and it's up to you to achieve and attain them. I felt like the most blessed man alive, and my confidence was boosted through the roof. When you get confidence, people can just see it in your attitude. With a good attitude, you will attract people to you, and when that happens, your network starts to grow. I always believe that if people associate themselves with people with good attitudes, they will also have a good attitude. If you choose to surround yourself with people with a negative attitude, then you will be negative.

Susan wanted to start a tradition of having Thanksgiving Day at our place. She's a great cook, and anyone who has ever eaten at our house always comments on her cooking. Trust me, this Thanksgiving we had a lot to be thankful for. I went to work the following Monday, still crossing out days on my desk calendar and counting down when my daughter was going to be born. Thinking that I was going to be a father was the most joyous feeling that I couldn't describe. All I knew was I was walking on air, and life had put me on the right track to accomplish what was meant to be accomplished in my life. I usually went to lunch from 1:00 to 2:00, but this particular day my supervisor asked me to go to the 28th floor to the big conference room. I was a nervous wreck because I was never called up there, so I was very concerned. My supervisor told me that he was going to come with me into the conference room. Now I was really worried because I had thought I had made a huge mistake. My supervisor and I took the elevator from the 17th floor to the 28th, and I asked, "Do you have any idea why I am coming up here?" He looked at me with a stern face and just said, "No." Wouldn't you know that from the 17th floor to the 28th floor, we stopped on every floor? The weird thing was no one was waiting for the elevator—we stopped on every floor, and no one came on. Finally, we arrived on the 28th floor, and my supervisor told me to wait. I started to sweat bullets, I lost my appetite, and tried to think what I did wrong at work, but I couldn't come up with anything. My supervisor came back and said, "We are ready." As we were walking to the conference room, I noticed there were a bunch of people in the room. When I opened the door, everyone yelled out, "Surprise!!"

I walked in and I walked out. I couldn't contain the tears flowing down my face. Here I thought that I did something wrong and was going to get in trouble for it, but it was a baby shower. Being a guy, I never thought a guy would get a baby shower; usually, it was the lady. I was excited, but most of all, I was relieved. My coworkers did a wonderful thing for me that day. My supervisor even gave me the rest of the day off.

Susan was not much of a fish eater; however, when she was pregnant, all she craved was tuna and salad, with Good Seasons Dressing. She ate those four times a day, and she enjoyed every bite that went into her mouth. She looked beautiful being pregnant. I was amazed that my dream of being a father was going to be a reality. During the eighth month of her pregnancy, she was bedridden. She took the couch, and I took the bed. I told her I would take the couch, but she insisted because she was out of work, and I had to go to work the next day. The baby was due on March 6, and it was still February—still a month away. At work, I was still counting the days on my calendar. To me, that month was a pretty long month, especially when you are anticipating the greatest prize in life: the birth of a child. One Sunday, we went to Susan's parents' house, and her mother called me to Susan's old bedroom and showed me a crib. She told me that it used to be Susan's crib. It was beautiful. Susan was an only child, and her parents had preserved her crib. My in-laws kept that crib at their house because we already had one at our place.

My father's birthday is on March 14, and I thought that maybe the baby was going to be born on his birthday. According to the doctor, Susan still had twelve days for our daughter to arrive. The next week started like a normal week. Susan was looking more and more beautiful each passing day. The week flew by, and the next thing I knew, it was Friday, March 19. I came home, and Susan was resting on the couch. Being Catholic and following the Catholic tradition, we needed godparents, so we talked about that. I picked my brother Thomas as my daughter's godfather. I wanted to return the favor because when his son Jacob was born, Thomas picked me to be Jacob's godfather, so out of respect, Thomas was my choice. Susan wanted Isabel, my uncle Antonio's widow, to be the baby's godmother. We had dinner. I forget what I had, but I do remember what Susan had: tuna, salad, and Good Seasons dressing. We watched a movie and just counted the blessings that were about to happen. On Saturday, March 20, we got up at a normal time, and Susan made breakfast. It was a time to spend time together, just the two of us. I actually did some housework, which was impressive in itself because I usually didn't do housework, but given Susan's condition, I was more than willing to do what I could to help. Susan's parents came over and we had lunch, they stayed a couple of hours, and then left. Susan was tired and she rested on the couch. It was close to suppertime, and I asked her if she wanted her tuna, and she said she wasn't hungry. She felt different, so she called her mother, and her mother and father came right over. Susan also called her doctor, and she told her it was time to come to the hospital.

At 6:30 p.m. on Saturday, March 20, we were off to the hospital. Susan's mother drove, Susan was in the passenger's side, and my father-in-law and I sat in the backseat. Her doctor was waiting for us at the hospital and took Susan into the room to examine her while my father-in-law, my mother-in-law, and I were in the waiting room. The doctor came back and said, "We are getting a room ready for her; we are going to keep her." We were all excited, especially me, because all my life I had waited for this moment, and finally that moment has arrived. My father-in-law stayed in the waiting room while her mother and I went to see Susan. She was a little nervous but excited and was resting comfortably. I gave her a kiss. The doctor said it was going to take a while, so I went back down where my father-in-law was, and I explained to him what the doctor said. He turned around and said, "It's going to be a long night," and went to buy coffee. He brought the coffee back and said he was happy he was going to be a grandfather. I was going to see Susan up in her room, and I asked him to come up with me. He declined. I asked, "Why?" He told me it was out of respect for his daughter. The time was going so slowly that I fell asleep while my father-in-law kept awake.

I woke up at 12:30 and told him I was going to check on Susan and for him to go to sleep, and if there was anything new, I would let him know. He agreed. He looked tired and said to me, "You belong with your wife." Deep down, I felt bad because I didn't want to leave him alone, but he was right. I went into the room. Susan's mom was sitting in the chair, and Susan was resting comfortably in bed. By this time, I was so excited to see the doctor. She came in and checked on Susan, and everything was fine. The doctor looked at me and said, "Why don't you get some rest?" I said, "I can't, because I am so excited and nervous at the same time." She said she understood, and then gave me a big hug and said, "You will make a great father." Susan fell asleep, her mother was resting on the chair, and there I was, wide awake. I went to check on my father-in-law, and he was sleeping, so I went outside into the bitter cold. I started to think about life after my daughter was born. It was a great feeling knowing that at any moment my daughter was going to be born, and everything I had always wanted and everything I had always dreamed about was about to happen.

At 4:30 a.m., I walked back into the hospital. My father-in-law was awake. He got us some coffee and started talking to me. He said, "I am glad that you are my son-in-law. You have been through a lot, but nothing stopped you, and you kept on going." At 5:00 a.m., the nurse came in looking for me and said, "It's time!" I looked at him and said, "I have to go!" He hugged me and said, "So go!" Back in the room, the doctor was there checking on Susan, and everything seemed fine. When I saw the head come out, I started weeping with tears of joy. I couldn't stop. My daughter, Brianna Marie Ferreira, was born at 5:25 a.m., weighing 5 lbs., 7 oz. That was the greatest miracle that God could ever give to me. That was the last masterpiece that I could ever create on earth: my daughter. The greatest living form that we call life. I finally saw the greatest miracle in my life. The miracle that I had been searching for all my life wasn't big; it was just 5 lbs. and 7 oz. Susan stayed at the hospital for a couple of days. During the last day, my company bought dinner for my wife and me. Compliments of Edwards & Angell: A nice steak dinner with all the trimmings and a bottle of wine.

40

Susan came home with our bundle of joy, and I went to work that following Monday, still on a natural high about the miracle that had occurred over the weekend. My coworkers were very excited for me. They saw that look on my face of being a proud father and the love that I had for my family. Susan stayed home for eight weeks while recuperating from giving birth. When Susan went back to work, she and I had a long talk about who was taking care of the baby on Saturdays while she worked. Every hairdresser knows that Saturdays are where they make the most money. During the week, Susan decided to take Brianna to her parents' house, and it made sense. But I started to get angry with myself simply because I couldn't take care of my own child on Saturdays. I totally understood, but deep down, I wanted to take care of my own child, and because of my cerebral palsy, I could not. The first time was the most difficult; Susan packed up everything and left to go to her parents' house. They drove away, and I was alone, crying because I couldn't take care of my own child. Susan was right—I couldn't pick her up to comfort her, or even change a diaper, or even feed her. Susan saw the sadness in my eyes and suggested that I come with her to her parents' house and stay with them while she worked. I declined, because while she was working, I could straighten out the house. I guess deep down in my heart, I thought if I couldn't do it right, I didn't want to do it at all. Simply put, my ego got the best of me during Brianna's early months on earth. I missed out because I was too stubborn to change the way I thought, instead of just being with my daughter on Saturdays when I could have been. Why is it that we as humans are never satisfied with what we have?

As Brianna got older, I told Susan that I would like Brianna to be at my parents' while she was working. She thought it was a great idea because her parents watched Brianna all week. My father would come down at 9:00 a.m., and my brother Michael would drop Brianna and me off at Susan's parents' house at 3:30 p.m. while we waited for Susan to come home from work. Fifteen years later, a lot has happened in my life and to the people around me. I left Edwards & Angell because the medical insurance got to be too much of a burden. I will always be grateful to them because, through the years there, I found out about my inner self and the person that I was intended to be. Leaving there was one of the hardest decisions that I have had to make. When I went to Human Resources, I cried like a baby because deep down I didn't want to leave, but I had to. I found another great job working for the State Department of Rhode Island in the Division of Unclaimed Property.

I got hired on May 27, 2001, and my supervisor, Richard Coffey, said, "I hope you like to travel because you are going to Myrtle Beach, South Carolina, in the last week of September." I smiled at him and thought, "What a wonderful birthday present," because my birthday was on September 29. Richard and I hit it off right away because he has a brother who's also disabled. September came around, and September 911 hit our country in a way that no one had seen before. Every American was devastated by what happened to our great nation. Of course, my trip got canceled. A lot of people died, and I often wonder why this had to happen. I don't think we will find the true answer until we meet our Creator. I pray every morning before I leave, and my last prayer is "Lord, let me see my family tonight because a lot of people didn't see their families that day." It was a needless act that should never have happened.

There were many stories that came out, but one stuck out and will forever be etched in my heart. A young lady just graduated from Harvard University, top in her class, got on the plane to Los Angeles to join a law firm to start on Monday as an attorney, but she never made it to her destination.

41

On October 14, 2003, my father-in-law passed away, and sadness took over. I enjoyed being with him because he taught me a lot, but now there was a void. I know Susan and her mother, Florence, took it hard, but I had a good relationship with him. He was a good man—always there for me when I needed someone to listen, and always there with a helping hand whenever I needed him. On November 9, 2005, my mother was hit by a car early in the morning. I got the call from my brother Thomas, and I was crushed. That changed my life; my favorite lady just got hit by a car, and I couldn't do a darn thing. It reinforced how important she has been in my life, and how precious our relationship is. The bond between us will never be broken, not even at the end of our lives. Three long months between the hospital and rehabilitation, and I never missed a day to go see her. I told my wife and my mother-in-law, "Forgive me, but I need to be with my mother every day at the hospital or until she gets home." They all supported me, so for the next three months I got up at 4 a.m., got home at 10 p.m., ate, kissed my wife, Brianna, and my mother-in-law, and went to bed. Only by the grace of God was I able to function, and to this very day, I don't know how I did it.

We have also come to find out that my mother has

dementia. Everything seems to happen to that poor lady, and I thank God that every day that goes by is another day that we have her. I have seen her age, and I wasn't ready for it. My father really does his best, but he needs some outside help. They found her an adult day care center. She seems to do well there, and of course, medication does help.

My brother Michael has been a blessing in my parents' lives. Besides working, he stops there every day, and stays a couple of hours. He lives closer to them and can spend a lot of time with them. My father gets frustrated, of course, because he wants to do more, but he can't. My mother-in-law passed away on January 8, 2006, with cancer. Susan and her mother had a very special relationship. It was pretty sad to watch my wife go through this, and all I could do was comfort her the best way I could. I wanted to do more, but I couldn't. Now, Susan's mother and father are both gone. It's just sad to see people that you love get sick or pass away, and you can't do a darn thing about it. On November 17, 2009, my uncle Manuel passed away from heart failure. It was sad, but his memory lives on. He was a good man whom I loved; he always encouraged me to go on and never give up.

My brothers are all doing great; we get together once a week. I just can't thank them enough for making me the person I am today. Even though I accomplished a lot, they were the key to my success, and no one can say anything different because it's the truth. They always pushed me to a new level, and they helped me to maintain the higher level. At times, it wasn't pretty, but I gave it all within my being to give. Michael, Thomas, and Victor, you three are the brothers that I couldn't even imagine having. I could never say too many thank-yous because without them, I would not be here today. I am entirely grateful to them. As for my daughter and wife, I will always be grateful to my wife for carrying my daughter for nine months and giving me the gift that God wanted me to have. I see it as a reward for meeting all the challenges that came and went, and by His Grace, I stood tall and withstood everything that came my way.

My daughter is in high school, an excellent student with a beautiful voice. She loves to sing. I am so blessed to call her my daughter, and I am proud to be called daddy. What more can a man ask for? As for me, every day I get up and my feet touch the ground, it's another day to share thet love that has been bestowed on me, and to bring a smile to people's faces so that they can see that my physical ability has not limited me, and that everything is possible without any boundaries. If boundaries pop up, it's important to take them head-on and do your very best. As long as you do that, knowing in your heart that was your very best, then you can smile and feel good. But if you take shortcuts, then those shortcuts will come back to haunt you.

Please learn from this man. I am very involved in my community, I never say no to speaking engagements, I am on the boards of directors, and I have my own website www.handicappedcommity.com. I am very active and am very happy in the direction I am going and with everyone in my life. I thank God that I have not allowed my disability to limit my life. In conclusion, please keep this in mind:

GOD + FAMILY + FRIENDS = SUCCESS.

Acknowledgments

1) I'm totally blessed to go to Meeting Street School, basically UI was and equal to my peers there. Ther teachers their top notch. They taught me your basic English, Math, and reading skill etc... They brought and developed my personality. How to behave with others, manner and how to be polite to others. If I had my way I would be 24/7, all students had some type of disability and that was the beauty that each one of us had. No one made fun of each other we were same boat.

2) When I got expected to collage, I cried simply because I never thought I never would it. I struggled going through college I was always behind as far as walking with peers, all of them tried to help me to carrying my books. Others took notes in class for me, When I fell someone was always to pick me up. I always had a guardian angel every day,

3) My last job with the state of Rhode Island was the best job I ever had. Paul Tarvas the 1st Treasurer that I worked under, I worked for the Treasury Department, There I had the best job ever, unclaimed property. They actually paid me to find your abandon property. It was a win, win situation. I had a wonderful co-worker who always helped to do my job better, Co-worker like, Robert, Kevin, Patrick, Betty, Geoge,

Mathew, Leah and Stacey. All of you I can't thank enough. Even though I don't see you every day you are in my- prayers. I want to thank my department and rest of treasury for giving me the best.

A special thank you to Emily Wilson and Deborah Catherine Faith.

Thank you,
Joseph

www.ingramcontent.com/pod-product-compliance
Lightning Source LLC
Chambersburg PA
CBHW050734010526
44107CB00010B/848